I0817468

'At a time when our world seems to be changing so quickly, when the uncertainty of the future can feel so overwhelming and I often want to hide away from marketing messages vying for our attention, Rachel's book is a gift! Her quietly wise words gently take us by the hand and remind us to travel with God through life to enjoy and protect his creation.'
Sarah P. Corbett, author of the award-winning *The Craftivist Collective Handbook*

'Join Rachel, a gentle guide to all things slow and intentional, as she prompts us to consider what really matters in life. Her lovely and thought-provoking book is one to return to throughout the seasons as we wake up to God's wonders around us. I can't wait to make the cheese and wild garlic scones …'
Amy Boucher Pye, spiritual director and author of *Transforming Love*

'With theological depth and quiet resilience, Rachel weaves her personal story of chronic illness, creativity and faith into a rich tapestry of slow living and spiritual presence. Her words are gentle, grounded and truly life-giving – a balm for the weary and a compass for those seeking a quieter, more rooted way to live with God. Thank you, Rachel, for all this hard-earned truth-telling, it was a gift to me and I know it will be to others too.'
Jo Hargreaves, The Faith-filled Therapist

'When did chronic busyness become normal? And what if we can no longer live at warp-speed for whatever reason? Rachel's writing and hard-earned insight help the weary soul to recalibrate, allowing us to rediscover rhythms, practices and mindsets that restore us physically and emotionally. This book is a much needed dose of wisdom for every season.'
Cathy Madavan, writer, speaker and author of *Why Less Means More*

'A gentle guide from a wise friend on seeking a slower pace amid a racing world with practical tips to help us make it a reality – comforting and challenging in equal measures.'
Rachael Newham, author of *Learning to Breathe*, *And Yet* and *Beloved Is Where We Begin*

‘In a culture that constantly demands we do more and more, this book invites us to step into the life of simplicity that Jesus offers and shows us the joy of finding more in less.’
Dr Jon Room, Pastor, Chipping Norton Community Church

Rachel Bearn was born and raised in the Wirral, UK. She studied for an Undergraduate Diploma in Creative Writing at the University of Oxford, and during this time began writing about sustainable fashion and lifestyle for Tearfund's online magazine, *We Are Tearfund.* After graduating, Rachel went on to work as a school library assistant but unfortunately had to leave after becoming very unwell. Rachel was diagnosed with ME and fibromyalgia in 2019. After a few years of learning to manage her chronic illness, she went on to study for an MA in Nature and Travel Writing at Bath Spa University. During the two years of study, she began to write professionally for many different national publications.

Rachel now works as a freelance writer for a number of UK bestselling craft magazines and as a content creator making videos for her YouTube channel, where she shares her handmade, homegrown and slow life.

A Christian guide to embracing handmade & homegrown

A YEAR to SLOW DOWN

Rachel Bearn

First published in Great Britain in 2025

Form
Part of the SPCK Group, Studio 101, The Record Hall, 16–16A Baldwin's Gardens, London EC1N 7RJ
https://spckpublishing.co.uk

EU GPSR Authorised Representative
LOGOS EUROPE, 9 rue Nicolas Poussin, 17000, La Rochelle, France
Email: Contact@logoseurope.eu

British Library Cataloguing-in-Publication Data
A catalogue record for this book is available from the British Library

ISBN 978-0-281-09113-3
eBook ISBN 978-0-281-09112-6

1 3 5 7 9 10 8 6 4 2

Typeset by Fakenham Prepress Solutions
First printed in Great Britain by Clays Ltd

eBook by Fakenham Prepress Solutions

Produced on paper from sustainable sources

To all those struggling every day with chronic illness who feel forgotten and alone. I hope you know how much value you have and just how much you are loved.

And to my husband, who never let me be forgotten.

Contents

Contents

Preface

> Make it your ambition to lead a quiet life: you should mind your own business and work with your hands, just as we told you, so that your daily life may win the respect of outsiders and so that you will not be dependent on anybody.
> (1 Thessalonians 4:11–12)

Handmade, homegrown, slow. I typed those three words into my Instagram bio. This little 150-character section of my social media had been the bane of my life for years: how to sum up what it is you are trying to do; what you are trying to create and the message you want to convey.

I started my Instagram and blog back in 2015 in a bid to share my journey into a slower pace of life. I was at university on a degree course I wasn't enjoying, and cracking under the weight of trying to live up to all of society's expectations of what a girl like me should be doing with her life. It all just felt so wrong. So fast. So … in your face. The things I was told would make me happy only seemed to make me more stressed and more tired. I knew I wanted something different. And that is when I found the slow-living movement.

It isn't clear exactly when the slow-living movement started, but we do know that it is a development of the slow-food movement started in Italy by Carlo Petrini in 1986 as a protest against the first McDonald's opening in Rome. Since then, we have also had the slow-travel movement and the slow-fashion movement. All of them are similar in their fight to slow down an ever-quickening lifestyle. People have recognised the ridiculous pace at which we live our lives, eat our food, travel and buy our clothes. They can see the negative effects it has on both us and the planet. So the movements to slow everything right down have begun.

At the age of twenty-one, as a fairly new Christian and a young woman desperately trying to figure out how to live as an adult, I found solace in the slow-living movement. I found a way of life that seemed to fit with so much of what I was reading in the Bible. I saw how Jesus chose to take time away, to be by himself, to enter the wilderness and to pray in gardens. I read how God wants us to 'not worry about your life, what you will eat or drink; or about your body, what you will wear' (Matthew 6:25) and I could see the benefits of living in the present moment, taking our time and simplifying as much as possible. I aspired to lead this slower life for many years, but it wasn't until aged twenty-four that I was forced to slow down.

I remember the morning I woke up in so much pain I couldn't move. My knees had been causing me problems for a few years by then, but this was different. I had pain all over my legs and I could barely stand. I called in sick to work that week, saw my GP and was soon referred to a specialist hospital. I had no idea then that I wouldn't be returning to work again; that the pain and illness would only get worse.

I spent most of 2019 housebound – stuck in bed or on the sofa in too much pain to move and with too much fatigue to try. I was diagnosed with myalgic encephalomyelitis (ME), or chronic fatigue syndrome (CFS), and fibromyalgia about six months after that first morning of pain in 2018. I had been through test after test and tried many treatments, all of which only seemed to make me worse. It got to September 2019, and I realised that enough was enough. I couldn't do it any more. No more treatment, no more tests and no more doctors.

I was depressed. I'm not sure it's possible to lose your entire life at twenty-four to illness and not become depressed. I was angry with God and couldn't understand why he was letting this happen. Why wasn't he helping me? Didn't he care enough to heal me?

I spent my days slumped on the sofa watching endless TV. One of the symptoms of ME/CFS is something called brain fog, which makes it very difficult to concentrate on anything, so I very quickly lost my ability to read books. My usual habit when I had nothing to do had always been to sit and read for hours and hours, but I couldn't concentrate on the words. I would lose my place, read the same sentence over and over again and get increasingly exhausted. It was no longer a safe place for me. But I couldn't just keep watching TV all the time. I needed something else to sustain me.

Before becoming unwell, I had been toying with the idea of learning to make my own clothes in a bid to be more ethical and sustainable, so

I decided that now was as good a time as any to pick up my knitting needles. And so my journey to living a handmade, homegrown and slow life began. Learning to knit helped to give my days some purpose and focus, I earned a little bit of money making baby cardigans for friends and family, and I had a way to express my creativity.

I began to share my journey on Instagram and soon found a wonderful community of makers, many of whom were Christians and some of whom even had chronic illnesses like myself. A few years later, when I learned to manage my ME a little better, I began to grow some food in my back garden. I started with a few pots of tomatoes, some salad and a hanging basket of strawberries. Getting outside more and growing food helped to bring me closer to God. It taught me to accept my lack of control and just take each day as it came. I could plant the seeds, water them, put them in the sun, but ultimately it was out of my control, and I simply had to trust.

A year later I began to sew my own dresses, something that would completely change my confidence level, as I was able to make clothes to fit my ever-changing body (thanks to chronic illness). I could source ethical and sustainable fabrics, and even use fabric waste for other projects.

My days became slow and quiet. Instead of constantly focusing on trying to get better, I focused on the tasks at hand and didn't worry too much about the future. I found great solace and inspiration in the 'cottagecore' aesthetic as it grew in popularity on Instagram. I was encouraged by these amazing creators to romanticise the everyday: to drink tea out of a vintage cup in the garden, to relish the glow of a candle in the evening as I knitted another cardigan, to enjoy the feel of a well-worn and comfy dress I had made. To take an ordinary moment and be grateful and thankful for it. It was a light in the darkness of pain and chronic illness. I continued to hope and pray for healing, but I trusted God that his plan was greater, and I was grateful for all he had given me in the pain and sorrow.

It wasn't long before I began to get better. Not better, better. I am still unwell; I still have low mobility, and pain is still an everyday part of my life. But this simpler, calmer way of life helped me to manage my illness; to calm my nervous system and focus my days on the present moment. It helped to remind me what was important: God and his plans. And trusting him always.

There's a better way

I don't know what you are going through. You could be chronically ill like me. You could be struggling with a mental-health issue or simply burnt out by modern life and feeling totally lost. Your life could be relatively straightforward or over-complicated. You could be someone living in the countryside or in the middle of a city. You could feel that life is going pretty well right now but you're missing a little something you can't quite put your finger on. God is here for that. For all of that.

I want to be very clear at the beginning that this is not a book about handmade, homegrown living *and* God. It is not even a book about God *and* slow living. It's just about God. God is all you need. He is the one who gets us through our days. He is the one we can rely on and trust and live for. James 4:8 tells us, 'Come near to God and he will come near to you.' Living a handmade, homegrown and slow life can be a means by which you connect with him in your everyday life and allow him to draw near just as he always promises to.

This is a way of living that reminds us of what truly matters in life. It encourages us to take the time to enjoy the everyday and the mundane in a fast-paced world of excessive consumerism where everyone seems to be shouting at us for more and more and more. More work, more money, more success, more house, more clothes. Slow living pushes all of that aside. It tells us to focus day by day, moment by moment. It encourages us to put our phone aside and read a library book instead. To take a walk in nature in a favourite dress worn soft and comfortable with age. To cook a meal from scratch and focus on the task in hand, leaving our racing mind and worries behind.

In 1 Thessalonians 4 there is some guidance on how to live to please God: 'make it your ambition to lead a quiet life: you should mind your own business and work with your hands, just as we told you, so that your daily life may win the respect of outsiders and so that you will not be dependent on anybody' (verses 11–12). A quiet life. One where we work simply and steadfastly for the Lord, trusting in his provision each day. This is what God wants for his children. And this aligns so well with what slow living stands for. On the outside it may just look like a romanticised aesthetic fit only for the Instagram highlight reel, but dig a little deeper and you will see the collective need for a slower and simpler way of life.

This isn't about moving to the countryside and buying an estate or a farmhouse. It's not about owning more or doing more. In fact, it's not about where you live at all. You could be in the countryside or the city; you might have quite a bit of disposable income or be struggling to get by each day. You might have lots of the skills we will talk about in this book already, or you may just be starting your journey. Slow living is something we can all incorporate into our everyday lives, wherever we are. In Hebrews 13:5 it says, 'Keep your lives free from the love of money and be content with what you have, because God has said, "Never will I leave you; never will I forsake you."'

Living slowly each day is a helpful way to remind ourselves of that truth about God: that he will never leave us. It is about being present in the here and now and relishing all the simple joys of the mundane and making the most of what God has given us. Slow living has helped me to learn true contentment in all circumstances as I lean on God. So I hope this book can help you too to slow down in this busy world – to focus on what is truly important. I hope that as we go through the different layers of a handmade, homegrown and slow life it inspires you and encourages you to find new ways to connect with God and faith.

Remember that this is not about giving yourself more to do. If you find you are putting pressure on yourself to live a certain way, remember to come back to the one who knows and loves you – the one who will guide you always. This is simply a way to connect with him.

Each chapter will have ideas for slowing down that you can incorporate into your life, wherever you are right now. You can skip to the season or chapter that works best for you at this moment, or start from the beginning of the book and make your way through. Go slowly. Try things out and don't put any pressure on yourself. There is no 'right' way to do things. You work out what works best for you and your relationship with God. I hope this book will be a source of inspiration and encouragement as you begin or continue on your journey to living a handmade, homegrown and slow life for him.

Much love,
Rachel x

WINTER

Early nights,
frost-bitten mornings,
tiny bulbs just beginning to poke out of the soil,
the red breast of a robin against a crisp blue sky,
evenings by firelight and candle,
crafts, books, baking, puzzles,
and time to hibernate.

1
Slow down

Adopt the pace of nature: her secret is patience.
(Ralph Waldo Emerson, *Nature*)[1]

Before I was ill, New Year was a full-on Bridget Jones moment for me. I wanted a Mark Darcy, a new diary and a list of resolutions that I would 100% stick to and they would transform my life. They usually centred around writing a bestseller, losing weight and saving all my money so I could travel the world. I would throw myself into January at a pace that was completely unsustainable. I normally allowed myself 1 January to enjoy with friends and family (although this did stress out my type A personality, which loves a 1st of the month or a fresh-start Monday to begin new things), but come 2 January, I'd be on it.

And sometimes I stuck to a few of those resolutions for a while. I often made it to early spring before they began to peter off. But most of the time I was fed up by 15 January. I think one of my biggest failures was my determination to try Veganuary, only to find myself eating sausages (not veggie ones!) by 10 January. But every year I would still set those goals and throw myself into January all guns blazing. The previous year didn't matter. This would be the year that everything would change. The best version of myself would be realised and all my wildest dreams would come true.

Fast forward to New Year 2020 and all that was gone. I had been sick for more than a year. I had been forced to leave my job, give up all my hobbies, and we hardly had enough money coming in to cover the bills, never mind save anything. My only goal for 2020 was to get better. To be well again. It's a common saying that you don't know what you've got until it's gone. And often those of us who have struggled with our health come to the stark realisation that all that really matters in life is good health. Becoming chronically ill takes you back to the most basic human needs and desires. Simple health. That is where it all starts. And for me that starts with slowing down.

I would like to preface this by saying that living slowly cannot make you better. If you are living with mental or physical health issues you will know that medical attention and proper treatment are necessary. But slowing down can improve symptoms and it can also help you to manage them. And that doesn't just go for those of us struggling with health issues. Millennials are being dubbed the burn-out generation – the ones who feel exhausted just by being alive in this loud, over-stimulating and intense world. This feeling of exhaustion inevitably leads to physical and mental health issues if we don't take action. It is time to find a better way of doing life.

He rested

> By the seventh day God had finished the work he had been doing; so on the seventh day he rested from all his work. Then God blessed the seventh day and made it holy, because on it he rested from all the work of creating that he had done.
> (Genesis 2:2–3)

I know many of you will probably be thinking, 'But Rachel, I can't rest. I have a family, a job, a marathon, a dog, a book to write …' We all have reasons why we can't rest. I've been writing and talking about slow living for years and regularly get the response: 'That's all very well and good for you, but I couldn't possibly.' We often believe our lives are harder than others'; that if people could only see what we actually have to do each day they might understand.

But the reality is that we live in a broken world, so we all have our struggles. We all have our difficulties. And we all have different levels of what we can and can't cope with. I am pretty sure, however, that none of us are quite as busy as God was at the beginning of Genesis. He had just created the earth, the waters and the land, all the animals and plants far too numerous for us ever to count. He was sovereign over all creation. He had a lot to do, yet 'he rested from all the work'.

God knows and understands the importance of rest. He created the human body to need sleep to give it time to recover, to grow and to heal. He created the seasons where working the land took up many hours in the day, giving us extra daylight and good weather to get it done, followed by quiet seasons of darker nights and colder weather drawing us into our homes to rest and recover.

He rested, and so can you.

Hibernation

When disability forced me to slow down, I began to realise how unintuitive the 'new year, new me' thing was. At this time of year all of nature is sleeping, lying dormant under frosty soil and waiting for the warmth of spring to bring it out again. But we as humans are waking ourselves up with false electric lights at 6 a.m. and forcing ourselves to achieve, achieve and achieve more.

It wasn't always this way though. Before electricity, January was the slow month, the time filled with frost and snow and little work to do on the land. This was the time to enjoy the fruits of your summer labour. To cook food from the store and pantry. To sit in front of the fire. To do the mending and the sewing. To knit socks, read books and most importantly let your body rest.

God created the four seasons to allow the plants of the earth to thrive. They cannot grow twelve months of the year, every year, for all of time. They must have time to sleep and lay dormant before reaching out and starting life all over again. Abscission, the loss of leaves or fruit from a tree, is a natural and important part of life. The sap, the tree's life force, is pulled inwards, away from the leaves and branches and back in towards the ground, causing the leaves to change colour, die and eventually fall off. Trees use minimal energy to survive the winter, storing and waiting for a better time of year. The trees hibernate.

Animals do this too. Here in the UK, many hedgehogs, mice, shrews, voles and bees will be hibernating – staying warm and cosy in the nests and homes they lovingly built in the warmer months. It is the natural cycle created by a perfect Creator.

Sadly, as humans we've lost our connection with the seasons, with nature's rhythms. The constant pulsating beat of the modern age telling us that we need more, more and more forces us from our homes and into a falsely lit January. If you often feel blurry-eyed and totally out of it at this time of year, believe me you are not alone. Perhaps you struggle to get out of bed in the morning. It may not surprise you to know that in winter many of us actually need one or two more hours of sleep a day. Our bodies are crying out for rest and hibernation.

Obviously, we have to go to work. I know many of us will be working outside of the home, and many people will be doing shift work, with their lives defined by set hours. You might be thinking, 'Yeah, hibernation sounds great, but how am I supposed to pay the bills?' I hear you. I am definitely not suggesting we all stage a coup and force the government to give us the whole of January off (although that does sound pretty epic, right?). I just want us to start thinking differently about January. Perhaps this month of pressure and resolutions could in fact be approached from a different angle.

Reframing achievement

For years now I have been having treatment for chronic illnesses. One of the first things we had to do at the clinic I attend is figure out which personality type we were. I am no scientist or doctor, but my own understanding of this was that nearly all people with chronic illness fall into one or more of five personality types. All five of these personality types are great when the person is operating mindfully, but when left unchecked they have a tendency to take our nervous systems to a place of high stress, where we can't possibly cope and inevitably end up seriously unwell. If you'd like to read more about this, I highly recommend Alex Howard's book *Decode Your Fatigue*. You can find details of this book, and others, in Resources at the back of this book.

I was very quickly assessed as an achiever. Achievers are people who find their life's purpose in their achievements. It often stems from a childhood of feeling the need to achieve for attention or affection. It very quickly became obvious that I was a type 1 achiever. I ticked every box. My entire identity and self-worth were wrapped up in how much I could achieve, from exercise goals, to hobbies, to career, to marriage. It was all about being the best of the best. And as soon as one goal was reached and achieved, I'd be on to the next, because I couldn't possibly live a life without achievement.

You might be able to see now why New Year's resolutions were such a big thing for me. But having this mindset not only put a huge amount of pressure and strain on my nervous system, it also meant that when things went wrong (as they inevitably do in life) my entire identity and reason for being alive came crashing down. The stress I was putting my body under was immense and it wasn't until I began treatment that I realised just how bad this had been for me.

And it wasn't just my body I was harming. I soon realised just how counter-Christian this was too. I had been a Christian for seven years at this point, yet I still hadn't learned the most fundamental part of our faith: you cannot achieve your way to God. Ephesians 2:8–9 says, 'For it is by grace you have been saved, through faith – and this is not from yourselves, it is the gift of God – not by works, so that no one can boast.' Jesus saved us, through his grace, through his love, through his sacrifice. Nothing I did would be enough. Which was why it never was. I could get every university degree under the sun, earn huge amounts of money and I would still never be happy, because this is not how God made us to be.

This can be a hard truth to realise, especially in a culture where we are taught to impress our parents at every turn. Making our parents proud is always wrapped up in what we achieve. It's wrapped up in the things they can brag about to their friends: the degrees, the jobs, the houses, the grandchildren. So when I viewed God as a father, it was hard not to apply the same logic. If I am honest, it still is really hard. But understanding that God's grace is all I need – that his grace is sufficient for me – allows me to dream instead of setting hard goals; to spend time chatting about my hopes with God. It allows me to think about the future and how I might go forward, but without the pressure of having to make it perfect or make it work, because ultimately I know that he will be with me always, no matter what I do.

I love dreams. I love having direction in my life. But God's grace takes away the stress and the pressure. It gives me freedom to follow him. I truly believe God gives us talents and skills and dreams for a reason. I truly believe the thing we dream of doing was most likely a seed planted by God. But knowing we are saved helps us to just go for it, without the pressure of having to succeed. We simply have to trust in him.

Dreams over resolutions

Now, don't get me wrong. Setting resolutions or goals is not bad. I often find it helps to look back at the year I've just had and begin thinking about the one I might like to have. But here's the thing: I'm not sure January is the time to do this. I realise that, naturally, we are going to be thinking about the new year. We can't help it. As humans we are desperate to know what's to come and we love to have a sense of control. And, as I say, New Year's resolutions are not all bad. If you're someone who finds them really helpful and your heart is in the right place – if you're using them as a tool to propel you forward in a healthy way and not put pressure on yourself – then great.

But I think most of us struggle to do that. January is a great time to let your body rest. To lean into the dark evenings of winter. To stay in. To have lie-ins whenever possible and focus on nourishing your body with delicious wholesome food while playing board games and doing crafts. January is also a great time to reflect and dream.

What do I mean by this? I suggest that instead of writing out a whole list of resolutions with a five-step plan for achieving each one, you have a bit of cosy time on the sofa or in bed with a notebook and pen, reflecting on the past year and dreaming about the year to come. Give yourself a good few hours to do this. I often find it helpful to do this on the afternoon of 1 January, when everyone is a bit sleepy from staying up late the night before and there isn't much to do but laze around in your PJs. Here are some questions you could ask yourself. It can be helpful to write down your answers.

- How do I feel about the year I've just had?
- What were the best parts?

- What were some of the most difficult parts?
- How do I feel my connection with God has been?
- Where can I see God's work in my life this last year?
- What do I feel about this coming year?
- What are the good things already planned?
- What am I worried about?
- What is a small dream I would like to see come true this year and what is a crazy big one? (You can write down as many of these as you like.)
- How can I connect with God this year?
- How do I feel God is leading me this year?

Take as long as you need to write your answers. Spend time in prayer, reading your Bible and meditating.

Routines

Having daily and weekly routines in place can help to slow your life down. I know that may seem counter-intuitive. Being forced to get to work at a certain time or do the school run on days when nothing seems to be going to plan can cause a huge amount of stress, and you find yourself rushing around. But this is where routine can help. Having a set bedtime and wake-up time each day, going through the same motions each morning to wake up your body and the same motions in the evening to put yourself to sleep, helps to regulate your nervous system. Regular routine creates clarity for your body, and it helps you to centre yourself.

The trick with routines is basically a 90/10 rule. For 90% of the time you follow the same routine, but you give yourself 10% wriggle room for the mornings when you aren't feeling great, when you're on holiday and routine has gone out of the window or when you're dealing with something a little difficult.

When I first started my morning and evening routines it was really hard. With chronic fatigue, starting anything new is hard. Every day I have to fight against the urge to just hole up in bed and sleep all day. My chronic pain causes my limbs to be so stiff it feels as though I can barely move. I know many of you will struggle with similar health issues. Maybe yours are less physical and relate to your mental health, but these can be just as debilitating, and getting out of bed each day is a real struggle. But this is where routines can help.

Having a regular morning routine means that when you wake up with that terrible feeling of anxiety, pain, fatigue and so on, you can simply focus on doing the first step in your routine. You just need to go through your normal motions. You can start that morning routine, stay completely in the present, and work out the rest as you go along.

Routine is also a great way to help your body to feel awake and ready to start the day. It will help you avoid that stressy half an hour in the morning when you run around trying not to be late for work, because you've planned just the right amount of time to do what you need to do. It will mean that you know the relaxation routine that is waiting for you when you get in of an evening and, on a difficult day, you can hold on to that all day to help you get through.

Circadian rhythm

You may have heard this term bandied around a lot in the last decade. Health gurus and TikTokers are often going on about resetting their circadian rhythm, but what does this actually mean?

The word 'circadian' refers to our biological twenty-four-hour cycle. Even in the absence of daylight these bodily rhythms occur, which is why when we fly halfway across the world we will find ourselves awake at 3 a.m., staring into the pitch black. There has been a lot of research done into our circadian rhythm and how we can use it to live better and healthier lives.

God created the twenty-four-hour day for a reason. The light and the darkness are both needed for the optimum health of the planet and for all living creatures.

> And God said, 'Let there be lights in the vault of the sky to separate the day from the night, and let them serve as signs to mark sacred times, and days and years, and let them be lights in the vault of the sky to give light on the earth.' And it was so. God made two great lights – the greater light to govern the day and the lesser light to govern the night. He also made the stars. God set them in the vault

> of the sky to give light on the earth, to govern the day and the night, and to separate light from darkness. And God saw that it was good. (Genesis 1:14–18)

Our circadian rhythm is the natural rhythm placed into our body by an incredible Creator who knows exactly what we need. When it starts to get dark, and we switch that big light off to put on a lamp instead and we do a giant yawn – that's our natural circadian rhythm. When the light comes streaming through the curtains and our body wakes us up before our alarm – that's our natural circadian rhythm. Our body knows what it's doing. So why aren't we listening?

The invention of the electric light bulb was incredible – an amazing display of the kind of scientific mind God creates. But it also has a lot to answer for. Before electric light was in every home in the UK, we were governed by the light and darkness in a day. And of course this was governed by the seasons. In the summer we would get up early, work hard all day, spend lots of time outside in the evenings and sleep less at night. In the depths of winter, we would wake late, work a little, get inside early and go to bed early. Our bodies were created by God to cope with this, which is why scientific study has shown it is normal for a human to need one or two hours' extra sleep in the wintertime.

With the invention of the electric light bulb, we no longer had to adhere to these timings. We could make it light all the time. We could get up and do whatever we wanted, when we wanted. Freedom! More productivity! More time? What should have been a great invention that led to greater freedom in the work and home space actually led to more and more and more work. It is now possible to do the same job twenty-four hours a day, so that is what our society chooses to do. Now we do not listen to our body's natural rhythms, we do not trust the inbuilt wisdom of our bodies that God created.

Getting started

When I first started thinking about my circadian rhythm, my body's natural clock, and how I could harness it to help me sleep better and hopefully begin to heal a little, I felt pretty overwhelmed. Completely shifting our morning and evening routines, adding in many things to remember, can be a lot. So please, take it slowly. Incorporate just a little bit at a time. And every few weeks, when you feel you've got your regular wake-up time sorted or your meditation is going well, maybe you can add something else.

Here are my daily routines to give you an idea of how you can start listening to your body more.

Morning routine

Wake up at the same time every day

Waking up at the same time is so hard in the beginning. Not so much during the week when you have to get up for work, but at the weekends when all you want is a long lie-in. I'm not saying you have to banish the weekly lie-in. I am such a fan of a lie-in, once in a while. But my body has begun to wake up naturally at the same time each day now, even at the weekends, and you know what? It feels good to just get up and go. It also means that in the evening, around the same time each night, my body is ready for sleep which, when you have a chronic illness causing serious sleep issues, is really helpful.

I understand that if you are a shift worker you will not be able to wake up at the same time each day. This is tough on your body. Go easy on yourself. Just aim to get seven to eight hours of sleep and wake up at the time that works best for you. My biggest suggestion to help the morning (or afternoon or evening) slump is simply to get up and get on with your routine. You can still incorporate much of this, and it will help your body.

Bible reading, prayer and meditation

I start each day reading my Bible, praying, journalling, doing a short breathwork meditation and taking in some morning light. Getting natural light on your face as early in the day as possible is really important for setting your circadian rhythm. I know this can be very hard in the winter when you're up early for work, but do what you can. If you're staying inside, the best way to get morning light is to open a window so you're getting it directly on your face. Again, this is difficult in the winter when it's cold, so if all you can manage is opening your curtains and watching the daylight start to trickle through, this is good too.

Meditation

'Meditation' is a word that scares a lot of Christians. It conjures up thoughts of New Age practices and other religions. But meditation is very biblical. We are regularly reminded in the Bible to meditate on God's word. In Joshua 1:8 God's people are told: 'Keep this Book of the Law always on your lips; meditate on it day and night, so that you may be careful to do everything written in it. Then you will be prosperous and successful.' The psalmist writes:

> Blessed is the one who does not walk in step with the wicked or stand in the way that sinners take or sit in the company of mockers, but whose delight is in the law of the Lord, and who meditates on his law day and night.
> (Psalm 1:1–2)

In fact, the whole book of Psalms encourages us to rest and meditate on the goodness of God; to allow ourselves to feel whatever we need to feel, be it joy or sorrow or anguish.

My morning and evening meditations have long been a space for me to work out my emotions with God: to read his word, to talk to him and to meditate on what he might have to say to me. Meditation is a great way to slow down, stay in the present moment and remember that God is in control.

You can do meditation anywhere you need to. I do mine at home in my bed, but I have friends who take time out of their day to do it in the office. It helps centre them if they are in a difficult and intense role. I tend to meditate each morning when I wake up, and I find this helps me to start my day right.

So, what exactly do I do?

Breathwork

A great way to begin meditation is to start with your breathing. Focus on breathing in and out. I will often count one, two, three, four, hold for two and then breathe out one, two, three, four, five, six. This helps to centre me and bring me into the present moment. Taking deep breaths automatically calms your body and the nervous system, so if your thoughts are flying around all over the place and you're feeling very anxious, I recommend starting with some breathwork. Just breathe as above and do it ten times, then see how you feel afterwards.

Affirmations

There is a lot of science around affirmations and how helpful they can be. An affirmation is simply speaking aloud a truth, or something you want to be true, during meditation. These days they tend to centre around the body's strength and ability. This can be very helpful for people living with chronic illnesses, addictions and mental health problems.

Personally, I find them very useful, but I like to tweak them slightly. My affirmations centre around God, and I often repeat Bible verses. This is where it can be useful to memorise Bible verses, although I am not the best at this so I often read them straight from the Bible and then meditate and repeat them slowly to myself with my eyes closed, keeping my breathing calm and slow.

Here are some affirmations to try:

- 'I am calm. I am present. I am surrounded by God's love.'
- 'My body is fearfully and wonderfully made.'
- 'I have nothing to fear because God is my strength.'
- 'I can do all this through him who gives me strength' (Philippians 4:13).
- 'But I will sing of your strength, in the morning I will sing of your love; for you are my fortress, my refuge in times of trouble' (Psalm 59:16).

Morning light

We've already looked at how morning light can be a great way to help set your circadian rhythm and tell your body it is time to wake up. Opening a window is a good start, but getting outside within the first hour of waking takes it one step further. If you have time for a morning walk, that is wonderful, but just standing for five minutes outside – in a garden, on a balcony or just on the street by your home or workplace – can make a difference.

Night-time routine

Going to sleep isn't always easy. I know from experience that bedtime can feel tricky for many living with mental or physical health problems. It's taken me years to get into a good sleep routine, but even with all the things I do to prepare for bed, I still struggle. My best tip is to try to get to sleep at a similar time each night. I know it's hard if you struggle from insomnia and I wouldn't suggest lying awake in bed for hours. If you can't sleep, get your book out again and have a read for a bit. But it can be very good for the body's circadian rhythm to have a regular bedtime. Essentially, a good night-time routine is like being a child again. Many of us grow up with such a great routine and thrive off it, but as soon as we become adults it all goes out the window. It's time to treat yourself as you would a toddler!

A quiet and slow night-time routine was a game-changer for me. Long gone are the days of staying up late watching TV. Now I treat myself like a six-year-old: bath, book and early bedtime! Especially in the wintertime. Of course, there will always be fun occasions when you want to stay up late, but for the most part an early bedtime can really help set you up for a successful day the next day.

This is the night-time routine I tend to follow:

No screens

My routine starts at 8:30 p.m., when I try to turn off all screens. This isn't always possible, but I do my best during the week to stop watching TV, stop looking at my phone and begin the wind-down for bed. It may not be the same time for you, but it is helpful to turn off screens at least one hour before bed. Our screens omit a blue light that tricks our circadian rhythm into thinking it's still daytime. Turning off screens can really help to signal to the body that it's time for bed, often resulting in a deeper, more restful sleep.

Taking a bath

I know they aren't for everyone, but I love an evening bath! A good soak in the tub is one of my favourite things to do. It can be a great way to soothe aches and pains before bedtime and it has become a big part of my chronic pain routine. I like to try to make my bath ritual as luxurious as possible.

Just because you do something every night doesn't mean it can't be special. Finding joy in the everyday is key to living a slow and simple life.

Try to keep the lighting low and relaxing, perhaps even try a bath by candlelight. I like to use some battery-powered lighting rather than the big bright fluorescent light we have in our small bathroom. I do not take my phone into the bathroom with me – I read instead. This really helps me to switch off and unwind, and I find myself looking forward to my soak and read every night.

You could try Epsom bath salts, great for achey muscles, and women in particular tend to be low in magnesium, which you can absorb in a salt bath. You could also try bubbles, bath oils, bath bombs and a lovely handmade soap. Upgrading your daily routines and making them extra-special is such an important part of self-care, so I encourage you to indulge.

Pray and journal

I like to end each day by praying. I often do this in bed, thanking God for what's happened that day and praying for what's to come tomorrow. I also take this opportunity to write down three good things from the day. I used to journal three things I was grateful for, but I found it easier to focus on little pockets of happiness and joy throughout my day. It can be as simple as the way the sunlight shone through the trees in the most magical way in the garden or having a roof over my head. It's a good reminder of the blessings of your day and helps to encourage you to notice them as you go.

Sabbath

> Then God blessed the seventh day and made it holy, because on it he rested from all the work of creating that he had done.
> (Genesis 2:3)

Many scientific studies have been done on the seven-day week. One study tried to elongate the week to ten days, but the results showed unhealthy levels of exhaustion in the study subjects. It is essentially accepted that a seven-day week, with at least one day of rest, is necessary for human life to thrive.

Of course, as Christians we know this to be true. Right at the very beginning of the Bible, God makes one day a week a holy day, a day of rest. But do we *actually* know this? It wasn't long ago that the only thing you could do on the Sabbath was attend church. No businesses were open, no food shopping could be done, no eating in restaurants. It was church in the morning, followed by either more church or an afternoon and evening of rest.

These days, with 24/7 opening hours and a culture that never stops, Sabbath has gone out of the window. It can be hard as a Christian not to become sucked into the convenience of Sunday opening hours; not to use it as an extra day to do the life admin. I know I am guilty of doing the food shopping or getting a vacuum out on a Sunday. But reading John Mark Comer's book *Garden City: Work, rest, and the art of being human* helped to reframe the working week for me. He says:

> That's why Sabbath is an expression of faith. Faith that there is a Creator and he's good. We are his creation. This is his world. We live under his roof, drink his water, eat his food, breathe his oxygen. So, on the Sabbath, we don't just take a day off from work; we take a day off from toil. We give him all our fear and anxiety and stress and worry. We let go. We stop ruling and subduing, and we just be. We 'remember' our place in the universe. So that we never forget … There is a God, and I'm not him.[2]

Sabbath is an important reminder of who God is. It is an essential part of the human make-up. A day of rest for everyone. It is a time to be with family and friends, to catch up on sleep, to eat delicious food, to watch a movie, read a book, do some crafting. And it is a chance to spend time with God.

I know that observing the Sabbath isn't always easy. If you're a mum or a caregiver, it can be very hard to feel as though you're taking a day off. But there are ways you can make this day more restful and special. Perhaps you could prepare a meal beforehand, so it just needs to be heated up. Maybe this can be the day you don't vacuum or do a load of laundry. Of course, your care duties, early morning wake-ups and nappy changes will all still be there, but maybe today you can share the load a little with someone else and cut out some of the extra things you do on the other days.

It is also important to note that Sabbath does not have to be on a Sunday. If you're a shift worker or a church worker, this day will be a normal day of work for you. In that case, it's important that you find another day in your week to practise Sabbath. The church workers in my life often take Saturday or Monday as a Sabbath. Find twenty-four consecutive hours a week where you can rest and worship God. Make it feel special, whatever that looks like for you.

Some who are reading this may be thinking that they already do most of these things, but for others this may all seem a bit overwhelming. That is totally okay. I get it. When I first started slowing down my routines and trying to take care of my body, it was a lot. As someone with chronic fatigue I wasn't sure how I could manage adding anything extra to my day. The trick is to simply pick one thing at a time. Perhaps you add in morning quiet time with God for just five minutes each day or maybe you try a short meditation each morning. After a while it will become part of your daily routine and second nature. At that point you could add in something else, like an evening bath or turning off your phone two hours before bed and reading a book.

Like everything this book encourages, take it slowly. There is no rush. You have all the time you need to make changes and incorporate them. Of course, you can do this at any time of the year, but winter is a great time to slow right down and try a new way of living. The days are short, the weather is cold, and staying in to nourish your body, mind and soul is just what your body is craving. Lean into these winter months and relish that time. Don't stress about resolutions or big goals. Just take your time to settle into another year. This is your year of slow and you have all the time in the world to get started.

Seasonal celebrations: Epiphany

After Jesus was born in Bethlehem in Judea, during the time of King Herod, Magi from the east came to Jerusalem and asked, 'Where is the one who has been born king of the Jews? We saw his star when it rose and have come to worship him.'

When King Herod heard this he was disturbed, and all Jerusalem with him. When he had called together all the people's chief priests and teachers of the law, he asked them where the Messiah was to be born. 'In Bethlehem in Judea,' they replied, 'for this is what the prophet has written:

"'But you, Bethlehem, in the land of Judah,
are by no means least among the rulers of Judah;
for out of you will come a ruler
who will shepherd my people Israel.'"

Then Herod called the Magi secretly and found out from them the exact time the star had appeared. He sent them to Bethlehem and said, 'Go and search carefully for the child. As soon as you find him, report to me, so that I too may go and worship him.'

After they had heard the king, they went on their way, and the star they had seen when it rose went ahead of them until it stopped over the place where the child was. When they saw the star, they were overjoyed. On coming to the house, they saw the child with his mother Mary, and they bowed down and worshipped him. Then they opened their treasures and presented him with gifts of gold, frankincense and myrrh. And having been warned in a dream not

to go back to Herod, they returned to their country by another route.
(Matthew 2:1–12)

Epiphany is the time in the church calendar when we celebrate the wise men, or Magi, visiting Jesus. It takes place twelve days after Christmas, falling on 6 January, and traditionally marks the end of Christmas in the Christian calendar. For many people in the UK this is still the date when all Christmas decorations are taken down and the last of the Christmas cake enjoyed.

But in the traditional Church of England calendar this day is more than just a reminder to put the baubles away. It is a time to reflect once again on the Christmas story, particularly the journey of the wise men. It is a time to remember that God's promises always come true and that he will always guide us back to himself. We need only look for him.

One of my favourite portrayals of the wise men is in the 2005 film *The Nativity Story*. The wise men are presented as early scientists, spending their days looking at the stars and the skies, trying to learn more about our planet. This is how I imagine them, spending years and years learning about the movements of the galaxies, seeing a promise in a star that is so special they set out on a journey that takes years.

The wise men had incredible faith. They knew something spectacular was happening, so they took all they had and travelled across continents to meet Jesus. Epiphany is a special time – a time to remember God's promises. To remember that he gave us his Son to save us. The busyness and excitement of Christmas may have gone, but the joy of Jesus is with us all year. Epiphany is a chance to enter the new year as we mean to go on, glorifying God, celebrating him and continuing to say, 'Yes, I want to be in relationship with you, Lord, all year.'

We seem to have fallen out of the habit of celebrating this festival here in the UK. But don't we all need a chance to remember God's amazing promises? Particularly in the cold darkness of January. I encourage you, then, this year to start a new tradition. One where you take down your decorations, tidy up the house and then celebrate Epiphany and all that God will do this year. Let it be a reminder that he is still the shining light that always guides us home.

Ways to celebrate Epiphany

Gather together

There is nothing better than gathering people together. Even if it is just you and your partner or best friend. It doesn't have to be a big gathering. Or you could invite your whole small group from church! Whatever works for you. But bringing people together marks the occasion. Make this a time to share a delicious meal and begin the journey into the new year as you mean to go on, in fellowship and community.

Light candles

This seasonal celebration is all about Jesus, the light in the darkness and the star that shone so brightly it brought three wise men across continents to find him. This is a great chance to light candles and remember the Light of our world. Why not eat by candlelight tonight? It is a truly special thing to do and will add an extra layer of magic to your evening.

Eat Epiphany food

Lots of countries have special food for this time of year. In France, there is a tradition of baking a galette with a small porcelain crown hidden inside. The person who finds the crown in their slice of galette is crowned king or queen for the evening. It's good fun, but I prefer the traditional Victorian Epiphany tart that we have in the UK.

Epiphany tart recipe

This is the simplest recipe in the world – I'm not even sure I am allowed to call it a recipe. It is perfect to make as a family with children or in a group. This can be made up on the night as part of the celebrations and baked to eat later on.

Ingredients

- 200 g plain flour
- 100 g butter, cut into small cubes and not too soft, plus a small amount for greasing
- Jug of water
- Assortment of jams
- 1 egg

Method

1. Preheat the oven to 200°C/180°C fan/gas 6 and grease a pie dish with butter.
2. Make the pastry: add the butter to the flour, rubbing it in using your thumb and fingers until it starts to look like breadcrumbs.
3. Add a very small amount of water to the mix and, using the flat of a dinner knife, begin to bring the breadcrumb-type mixture into the water. Keep adding a little bit at a time, mixing with your knife until it starts to form a dough.
4. Roll out the pastry into a large rectangle.
5. Cut 6 long strips off one end, about 1 cm in width. Put these to one side.
6. With the remaining pastry, roll it onto your rolling pin and then carefully unroll over the pie dish. Gently press it

into the dish, making sure it fits into the base, then trim off the excess around the edge.

7 Taking the pastry strips cut earlier, twist slightly and arrange inside the pie dish on top of the pastry base into a six-point star. You will need to trim some of them to make them fit into a star shape. If you don't have enough pastry, use the off-cuts from the pie dish.
8 Spoon jam into each section created by the star.
9 Beat the egg and use to lightly brush over the pastry.
10 Bake in the oven for 25 minutes or until pastry is golden.
11 Once cooked, remove from the oven and leave to cool completely and allow the jam to set.

Enjoy!

A prayer for Epiphany

Dear Lord

Thank you for the star that brought the wise men to Jesus. Thank you that you always provide the guiding light we need to find you. Thank you for giving us your Son, the Light of the world. As we say goodbye to Christmas and enter this new year, Lord, I ask that you will help us to seek you; that in the darkness of winter, we remember to look up and see you guiding us with your light. Would you bless this year for our family/ friends gathered here and would you keep bringing us back to you, Lord. May we never lose sight of you. Amen.

2
By hand

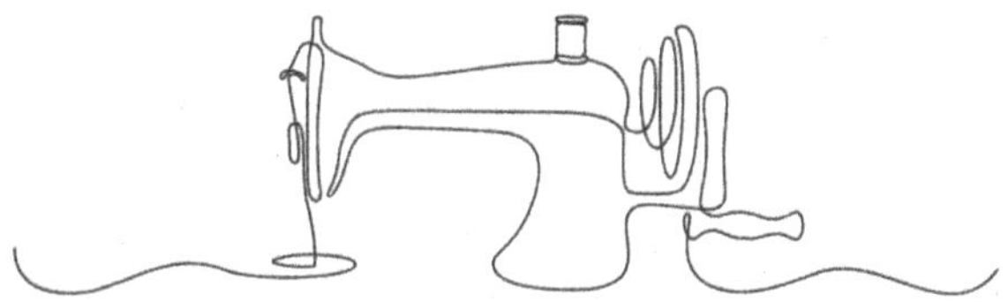

> Because man was created in the image of a creator. Man was created that he might create. It is not a waste of man's time to be creative. It is not a waste to pursue artistic or scientific pursuits in creativity, because this is what man was made to be able to do. He was made in the image of a creator, and given the capacity to create.
> (Edith Schaeffer, *The Hidden Art of Homemaking*)[3]

> ... and to make it your ambition to lead a quiet life: you should mind your own business and work with your hands, just as we told you, so that your daily life may win the respect of outsiders and so that you will not be dependent on anybody.
> (1 Thessalonians 4:11–12)

It wasn't so long ago that making things by hand was the norm. If you needed a new dress and didn't have the luxury of being able to afford to pay someone else to make it for you, then you made it yourself. It wasn't until the early twentieth century that we began to see department stores selling clothes 'off the rack'. It was a huge development in fashion history when clothes were no longer made to measure, ordered weeks in advance at great expense. Instead you could walk into a shop and buy a relatively affordable dress and take it home that day. But it marked the beginning of fast fashion, of clothes becoming more readily available, and the skills needed to sew a garment from scratch, to repair, sew on a button or breathe new life into something began to be lost.

Skills that were passed from generation to generation have quickly been phased out over the last century by the invention of quicker, more efficient machinery and globalisation. Many of the things we use today are in fact still made by hand, but someone else's hand, in another country, forgotten about and often exploited (see Chapter 4 for more on this).

But there is something special about working with your hands. Jesus himself spent half his life working with his hands. Before his ministry began at thirty years old, he was a carpenter like his father. A useful skill passed down from generation to generation. One that not only helped to house your own family but other families too, and would put bread on the table. I can only wonder at what the Creator of our universe was able to carve. Can you imagine living in a house built by Jesus?!

Learning to knit

When I first became chronically ill, I wasn't able to leave the house much. I was in a lot of pain and couldn't walk. I was struggling to come to terms with this new norm, unsure of whether this was for ever or simply a problem I needed to wait for the doctors to fix. My usual pastime of reading became too difficult due to the brain fog I was experiencing (disabling cognitive impairment), so I would spend hours and hours slumped in bed or on the sofa trying to distract myself from the pain by watching TV.

That was until I decided to learn to knit again. I had been taught how to knit as a young child at the age of about ten. I was staying with a family friend for the weekend and her parents had come to visit from India. Kamla was a formidable knitter; she would sit for hours knitting beautiful garments. I was fascinated by her ability to bring clothes to life on her needles, and I spent that weekend watching as her needles clicked and clacked and a long fluffy scarf began to appear.

I begged Kamla to teach me, but with no spare yarn or needles she could only teach me through showing me what she was doing. I watched in awe, desperately trying to absorb the skill. Later that week my auntie

Sarah came to pick me up and I talked her ear off about learning to knit. She offered to teach me and soon we were sitting in the living room with needles and yarn, and I was learning to cast on, knit, purl and cast off.

I would keep coming back to knitting over my teen years. I loved the idea of creating my own clothes, but I hadn't yet learned to read and follow a pattern. I have always been a very impatient person, so my approach was to pick up the needles and just start knitting, hoping for the best. But this meant I never really learned what I was doing until I was forced to slow down.

Sitting on the sofa, legs up and Hercule Poirot on the TV (David Suchet always) in an attempt to dull the pain, I picked up my needles again. This time I was in no rush. Instead, I chose a pattern from a magazine, bought the suggested yarn and began knitting. If you are a knitter or a crocheter yourself, you will be wincing at the fact that I didn't even make a gauge swatch. (This is when you knit a small patch in the design of the pattern to make sure your gauge matches that of the pattern. If you don't do this, the piece you're knitting can come out completely the wrong size and shape.) But at the time, I had no idea what a gauge swatch was or why I needed to make one! The jumper turned out lumpy and a bit messy in places. I had no idea how to mattress stitch (invisible seaming of knitted garments), so the seams were all bobbly. But it didn't matter. I had created something with my own hands. Despite the awful pain and fatigue, I had done something and to me it was truly beautiful.

Health benefits of crafting

Each day adding row after row after row kept me sane. I began to have something to look forward to, to work towards. I didn't know it then, but I was also helping to reduce my pain and calm my nervous system. Studies show that knitting and crochet can help to reduce chronic pain, particularly that of arthritis, and they have real calming effects.

In her book *Craft Psychology: How crafting promotes health,* Dr Anne Kirketerp writes:

> Craft is a well-known and natural method to create peace, joy and meaning. But many are not aware of the psychological mechanisms

> that deliver these benefits, and even fewer know how to use craft psychology in a modern everyday life to maintain well-being and soothe or counteract a range of negative emotions such as symptoms of stress, despondency and unrest.
>
> Indeed, we can buy factory-made sweaters and socks, bowls, and bread more cheaply, but still, we choose to knit, carpenter, and repair them ourselves. We throw our own clay teacups or graft apple trees; we make mosaics and weave flower wreaths. We do not need to make any of these things, but we do it anyway, because we have experienced the difference crafting makes. We know that it makes us more capable of dealing with life.[4]

Anne's book is filled with insight, knowledge and scientific research that shows the immense effect crafting has on the human body. I have shared details on the Resources page and would recommend you read this. I recently heard Anne speak at a knitting event and felt my earlier suspicions had been validated. I knew crafting had helped me immensely, and I knew that a few studies had begun to show the incredible impact of knitting on chronic pain, but Anne's research has shown that crafting can have a profound effect on the body and its ability to heal and cope with the difficulties of life.

Made to create

God is the ultimate Creator; he crafted the universe and every beautiful thing we see. In Genesis 1:27 it says, 'So God created mankind in his own image, in the image of God he created them; male and female he created them.' We are made in the image of the Creator, so our deep desire to create something with our hands is innate, and has been since the first day of creation. God delights in our making, in our crafting – he delights in us using our hands. Each time we create, we reflect the one who made everything. Is it any surprise, then, that more and more scientific studies are showing the health benefits of making with our hands? Of course it is good for us! It was designed this way by a perfect Creator.

But what if you're not creative? I hear this a lot from people who think they aren't creative in any way or don't have the ability to make things.

We are all gifted differently, but I believe that there is a craft out there for everyone, and that turning our hands to making something, even if it is just sewing on a button or baking a cake, helps bring us closer to God. It calms our nervous system, brings us into the present moment and helps us to focus on one task at a time.

> Therefore I tell you, do not worry about your life, what you will eat or drink; or about your body, what you will wear. Is not life more than food, and the body more than clothes? Look at the birds of the air; they do not sow or reap or store away in barns, and yet your heavenly Father feeds them. Are you not much more valuable than they?
> (Matthew 6:25–26)

Making with our hands forces us away from screens and busyness, and instead helps us to focus on the task at hand. We are called not to worry about our lives, to focus on one day, one hour, at a time, trusting God will guide us through. Making with our hands is a wonderful way to take care of our health and simply focus on the next task. It helps to slow down life, to take us back to the simple actions of moving our hands to create something that is unique, beautiful and cherished.

How to get started

There are so many stories in the Bible of God gifting people with the ability to make beautiful things for his glory. In Exodus 35 God commands the Israelites to create the tabernacle, the sacred space where God's Spirit will dwell: 'Every skilled woman spun with her hands and brought what she had spun – blue, purple or scarlet yarn or fine linen. And all the women who were willing and had the skill spun the goat hair' (verses 25–26).

Later in the same chapter we hear of how God bestows his gifts for creating on his people:

> See, the Lord has chosen Bezalel son of Uri, the son of Hur, of the tribe of Judah, and he has filled him with the Spirit of God, with

> wisdom, with understanding, with knowledge and with all kinds of skills – to make artistic designs for work in gold, silver and bronze, to cut and set stones, to work in wood and to engage in all kinds of artistic crafts. And he has given both him and Oholiab son of Ahisamak, of the tribe of Dan, the ability to teach others. He has filled them with skill to do all kinds of work as engravers, designers, embroiderers in blue, purple and scarlet yarn and fine linen, and weavers – all of them skilled workers and designers.
> (verses 30–35)

I truly believe everyone has something they can do or could be good at with some practice. If you're not sure where to start, perhaps ask God to help uncover the gifts and talents he has bestowed on you. Then just start having a go! Much like a good exercise routine, it is important to find the crafts that work for you. I've tried many crafts in my time, but only a few have stuck. I encourage you to keep having a go at different crafts until you find the right one. Here are a few tutorials to get you going.

Lavender soap

Making soap is really easy, so I have included a simple recipe here. There are many ways of making soap, but this is my go-to. I find it both cost-effective and satisfying to fill my home with homemade bars of soap.

Ingredients and equipment

- 1 kg melt-and-pour soap base
- 100 drops of lavender essential oil
- Dried lavender
- Grease-proof paper
- Loaf tin
- Saucepan
- Glass bowl that sits inside your pan but doesn't touch the bottom
- Water

Method

1. Chop the soap base into 1 cm cubes.
2. Heat some water in the bottom of your saucepan. Once boiling, turn down to a simmer and add the bowl on top.
3. Place all the soap cubes into the bowl and leave to melt, stirring occasionally.
4. Once the soap base is completely melted, take off the heat and add in 100 drops of lavender essential oil.
5. Line the loaf tin with grease-proof paper, then pour in the soap mix.
6. Add dried lavender to the top of the soap.
7. Leave to set for 24–48 hours.
8. Once set, cut into 8 slices and enjoy!

Beeswax candles

Ingredients and equipment

- 500 g natural beeswax pellets
- Saucepan
- Metal jug with plastic handle
- Essential oils (any scent you like – it is fun to experiment with flavour combos!)
- Wicks with stickers
- Wick holders
- Small pots, jars, tea-light holders – anything you can fill to make a nice candle

Method

1. Heat water in the saucepan. Once boiling, turn down to a simmer and put the bowl on top.
2. Pour wax into the jug and leave to melt, stirring frequently.
3. Once melted, turn off the heat and add in 10–20 drops of essential oil.
4. Stick wicks into the bottom centre of all your candle holders.
5. Slowly pour the wax into the holders, trying to keep the wicks straight through the middle as you do this.
6. Place the wicks in wick holders so they stay central as the candles set.
7. Leave to set for 24 hours.
8. Light and enjoy!

Braided basket

Equipment

- Old fabric scraps cut into strips
- Sewing machine
- Denim needle
- Sewing thread

Method

1. Begin by plaiting your fabric strips into a long braid. (The length of the braid will decide the size of your basket. You can see roughly how big it will be by creating the basket with your hands and holding it together.)
2. You can add in more fabric to your braid as you go by holding it with the piece that is going to run out. Simply braid it in for the last few centimetres of that piece.
3. Once you have enough braid, thread up your sewing machine with the colour you want, making sure you use a denim or hard-fabric needle. Set it to a large zig-zag stitch.
4. Fold the beginning of the braid down by about 3–4 cm so that it lies flat next to the rest of the braid. Sew this in place.
5. Slowly add braid round and round in a circle, sewing into place. You should start to form a disc.
6. Once the disc is as big as you would like the base of your basket to be, you will need to start manipulating the braid so that it begins to go upwards. Hold the braid slightly at an angle as you sew, to form the sides of the basket. This can be a bit fiddly, so take it slowly.
7. Once you've formed the sides, keep sewing in braid until you have the height you want.
8. Remember to keep the basket towards the left, so it has room to grow out and doesn't get caught in the machine!
9. Enjoy using your handmade scrappy basket.

Other crafts to try

- Knitting or crochet
- Dressmaking or quilting
- Punch needle
- Weaving
- Rag rugging
- Embroidery or cross stitch
- Needle felting
- Spinning
- Jewellery making
- Pottery
- Woodwork
- Furniture making/upholstery

Using craft for God's glory

Throughout history God has used the creativity and talents he gives individuals for his glory. We need only to look at beautiful stained-glass windows, embroidered banners in churches declaring his truths, or beautiful miniature Easter gardens created in churches around the UK at Easter time. Crafts have long been used to make a difference in this world, both inside and outside of the Church. A new word is being used for the type of activism where craft is used to create change: craftivism.

Craftivism

Talking to Sarah P. Corbett, who is a Christian, the founder of the Craftivist Collective and author of books *How to Be a Craftivist* and *The Craftivist Collective Handbook*, she told me more about her approach to craftivism and how it looks today:

> Craftivism is activism through craft. The word 'craftivism' was coined in 2003 by Betsy Greer as a 'way of looking at life where voicing opinions through creativity makes your voice stronger, your compassion deeper and your quest for justice more infinite'.
>
> There are many ways people interpret and do craftivism. I call the Craftivist Collective approach 'gentle protest'. I don't mean gentle

> as in passive or weak, but gentle as in gentleness being one of the fruits of the Holy Spirit: restrained behaviour towards others that is compassionate and correct in each nuanced context. Unlike many other forms of craftivism, my approach is slow, quiet, calm, focused, ego-less, hopeful and humble. Gentle protest craftivism is a form of soft power, appealing to and attracting audiences to social change. Sadly, there are forms of craftivism in the world that work within the 'drama-triangle' of victims, perpetrators and heroes' model that is not helpful in our complex world. I avoid craftivism projects that are motivated by revenge or self-aggrandisement, or only express anger without looking at how we can all be part of the realistic solutions and using craft to serve the cause.[5]

Sarah grew up in West Everton, inner-city Liverpool, in the fourth most disadvantaged ward in the UK during the 1980s. Her dad was the local vicar and area dean for over forty years and her mother became the local councillor and Deputy Mayor of Liverpool City Council. There is a photograph of Corbett aged three with the Bishop of Liverpool, David Sheppard, and members of her community outside social housing they squatted in, to successfully save from demolition. The houses are still there. She was brought into the world of activism as she experienced firsthand her community battling against the effects of inequality, and when she was eight, her family went to South Africa in 1991 to learn about the peace and reconciliation work of Nelson Mandela and Desmond Tutu as part of her father's sabbatical with the Church of England. At her secondary school she initiated a successful campaign to gain lockers for her peers and the use of recycling bins before they became mandatory. She went on to work for international development agencies, including Oxfam GB. But it was beginning a cross stitch on the train as a way to relax that first gave Sarah the idea to use craft as a form of activism:

> I immediately noticed when I was threading my needle how impatient I was, how shaky my hands were and how burnt out I felt. The calming and repetitive hand actions of sewing were empowering, gave me confidence and created a comfortable space for me to really reflect and pray on uncomfortable questions I had

been avoiding but were niggling at me, such as whether the activism I was teaching in my job or doing with activist groups in my personal life was effective, kind or burning me out. Plus an elderly couple opposite me asked me what I was stitching and I thought, 'I wish I was stitching a quote about inequality that we could discuss rather than sewing this teddy,' and then my first craftivism project idea came into my head: mini protest banners that are postcard-sized cross-stitch patches you hand out somewhere relevant to the issue you have stitched. So I Googled 'craft activism' and the word 'craftivism' existed. It all happened very organically and quickly on that train to Glasgow.

Since its creation in 2009, the global Craftivist Collective has helped change laws, policies, hearts and minds around the world, as well as expand the view of what activism can be. This quiet, compassionate and visually intriguing activism uses handicrafts as a tool for 'gentle protest' to help our world become more beautiful, kind and fair. My gentle craftivism actions won't change the world quickly or on their own: they have to be part of a wider activism strategy. We need to practise perseverance and pragmatism as craftivists, to see our efforts as seeds for thought, conversation and ultimately transformational change, in ourselves and hopefully in others. We need to create our craftivism with nuance and empathy, treating people how we want to be treated, whether they are the powerholder or those directly affected by injustice, and craft it to fit each context.

Craftivist Collective's 'gentle protest' craftivism approach is a combination of art and science. It is not art therapy or solely awareness-raising. See yourself and this community as 'design activists', weaving attractive colours with intriguing imagery, soft textures with foundations of thoughtful campaign strategies, contextual sensitivity with wisdom from protesters of the past, as well as insights from the fields of neuroscience and psychology. Our 'crafterthought questions' within every project I create are designed to help us think deeply, critically and compassionately on the issues, as well as be mindful of any presumptions and unconscious bias we might be stitching into our craftivism. It is challenging work. Yet you will see from the voices and images of members of the global Craftivist Collective throughout my books and on social media that the hard work and heart work in their gentle craftivism has been worth it to be the loving changemaker our world needs.

Activism can be slow

Before I became chronically ill and disabled, activism was a big part of my life. I organised my first fundraising event at ten years old, for the RSPCA, and I can't remember a time from that moment on when I wasn't campaigning for change. I ran a charities committee at my school, rang up Nestlé in my summer holidays to ask why they were buying cocoa beans from farms using child labour, I boycotted fast fashion in my early twenties and when I became a Christian at twenty the need to make change and speak up for those unable to speak up for themselves only increased.

Just before my illness started, I had begun speaking regularly to church groups and organisations about the ethical and environmental impact of the clothes we wear. It is a message I am very passionate about and I go into this in much more detail in Chapter 4. I had hoped to visit more groups, begin spreading the word and getting involved with charities that fight against modern slavery. My illness put a stop to all of this. Suddenly, I was unable to leave the house. I couldn't attend protests or campaign meetings, or do talks. I was sitting in my ethically made, sustainable PJs on the sofa feeling completely useless.

But this was when social media became my activism space. I had been writing a blog for years and sharing my views via social media, but now this was the only form of activism I was able to be involved in. It was quiet and slow, sharing the benefits of making clothes – on our nervous system, the planet, people and animals. I took part in crafting drives making clothes for Ukrainian refugees, knitting tiny hats for premature babies on the NICU wards and running a knit-along to raise money and awareness for Alzheimer's disease.

These forms of activism were done from my home. They were quiet and slow – something I could manage despite disability and illness. But they made a difference. Money was raised, questions were asked and people in terrible situations felt the kindness and love of a stranger in some of their darkest moments.

And it wasn't long before I was able to take some of this outside of the home. My husband and I ran a games and crafts night for a time in our last church. It wasn't a big, bright, shiny campaign, but it was something that could help combat loneliness in our community and perhaps help those struggling with mental health. We created a safe space where anyone could come and bring a craft. People could chat to someone, get some help with what they were working on or just quietly work on a craft with a group of people and feel less alone.

The great thing about craftivism is that it's accessible to anyone. You can do it even if you're disabled or unwell like me. You can do it if you're elderly. You can do it even if you don't speak the language or you're young.

In the church we attended when we lived in Chipping Norton, there was a young girl called Hope. This was a very apt name, because although she was only eleven years old at the time, she used her crafts to bring just that – hope. I was a recipient of one of her lovely cards. After going forward for prayer during a difficult period in my life I had found myself crying. Clearly Hope had noticed, and while I was being prayed for she made me a card with a Bible verse on it. When I got back to my seat after many hugs and tissues (you'll know the drill), I found it waiting for me. I almost started crying again! But it was just the reminder I needed. I put the card in my home office and for months found myself gaining strength by looking at that verse again and again. A small act of craftivism that made a big difference.

Ideas for craftivism

- Join a knitting drive. There are so many groups across the country looking for knitters to help them make clothes for premature babies, as well as blankets, teddies and much more. Have a look at The Warm Baby Project for more info.
- November knit-along. Many charities run a knit-along in the month of November to help raise money. Instead of doing a sponsored walk or run you can stay at home and knit. There is also the same for crochet.
- Cross stitch or embroider a Bible verse to give to someone.
- Make beautiful cards to encourage people.

- Sew, knit, crochet and mend your own clothes. In today's society this alone is a radical act of rebellion, helping us all to become more self-sufficient, and it's good for the planet.
- Organise a weekly or monthly craft group to help bring people together and combat loneliness.
- Use craft as a way of reaching out to refugees who may not speak your language. Perhaps you could learn a skill from someone else's culture.
- Sew banners, quilts or embroidery with phrases and depictions of causes that mean something to you. Put them up in your home to encourage conversations, or take pictures and share on social media.
- Make a gift for someone who is struggling.
- Make something for a new mum – perhaps something for the baby and something for her.

I hope this chapter has helped to inspire you to make with your hands. It is a wonderfully slow and simple pastime that can be used not only to benefit you and your nervous system but also help our planet and people. If you'd like more ideas on crafting, head to Resources for some helpful books, and links to my YouTube channel.

Seasonal celebrations: Lent

Then Jesus was led by the Spirit into the wilderness to be tempted by the devil. After fasting forty days and forty nights, he was hungry. The tempter came to him and said, 'If you are the Son of God, tell these stones to become bread.'

Jesus answered, 'It is written: "Man shall not live on bread alone, but on every word that comes from the mouth of God."'

Then the devil took him to the holy city and set him on the highest point of the temple. 'If you are the Son of God,' he said, 'throw yourself down. For it is written:

"He will command his angels concerning you,
and they will lift you up in their hands,
so that you will not strike your foot against a stone."'

Jesus answered him, 'It is also written: "Do not put the Lord your God to the test."'

Again, the devil took him to a very high mountain and showed him all the kingdoms of the world and their splendour. 'All this I will give you,' he said, 'if you will bow down and worship me.'

Jesus said to him, 'Away from me, Satan! For it is written: "Worship the Lord your God, and serve him only."'

Then the devil left him, and angels came and attended him.
(Matthew 4:1–11)

Lent is the period leading up to the celebration of Easter, the biggest event in the Christian calendar. It normally begins somewhere in February, or early March if Easter Sunday comes late in the year. For many, it is a time of quiet reflection and preparation, where time and body are devoted to God. The tradition that we most associate with Lent is the Lenten fast.

There isn't a huge amount known about the origins of the Lenten fast, but historians believe it can be traced back as far as 325 CE to the first ecumenical council of the Christian Church, the Council of Nicaea. The tradition of starting Lent with Shrove Tuesday, or Pancake Day, is said to have begun in medieval times, a good thousand years later, the idea being that before entering a time of fasting and thrift, you would use up all the good, yummy foods in the larder. Butter, milk, eggs, sugar and all manner of sweet things were used up before a period of austerity in preparation for Easter.

Today, many Christians still begin Lent with Pancake Day, often hosting pancake-tossing competitions at church and then spending the next six and a half weeks abstaining from something – for example, chocolate, crisps or meat – in devotion to God.

Fasting is an important spiritual discipline for those Christians who are able to do it. We find many instances in the Bible where people fast in devotion to God. But sometimes I worry that the tradition of fasting at Lent has lost some of its power. It seems that many see it as more of a diet than a real opportunity to give something to God. Not to mention it isn't always possible for those of us with health conditions to take part. So I propose that our fasting could look a little different.

One of the biggest barriers to God in the UK has got to be our busyness. I can't tell you how many times I've been simply 'too busy' to do my quiet time. And I know this is the case for so many others. I've had lots of conversations with friends, trying to figure out how we fit our Christian lives into our 'normal' lives. The world runs at a ridiculously fast pace, and it is so hard to find that balance.

Of course, there is no such thing as a 'normal life' and a 'Christian life'. It is all life under God. Everything we do can be used to glorify God. Getting to work on time, doing our job well, being involved in our friends' lives and spending time with family are all important parts of living as a Christian. The difference between whether this glorifies God or is a distraction from God is to do with our heart posture. Where is our heart as we do these things? Is it about glorifying God and living well for him?

Lent can be a great opportunity to remind ourselves of what is important; to slow down and refocus life on God. And if giving up chocolate is going to help you do that, then that is great. But if actually this year you would like to go deeper in your relationship with God and perhaps remove some of the barriers stopping you doing that, I'd like to suggest some alternatives.

Ideas for an alternative fast

Social media

This is a big one for many of us, isn't it? I will shamefully put my hand up and say that I am guilty of the doom scroll. I find it very hard to get the balance with social media, especially as it's such a big part of my job. It is one of the biggest distractions of our modern age. One minute we are just checking Instagram and the next we've been sitting for an hour watching video after video of greyhounds doing hilarious greyhound things (guilty as charged).

Social media can be a great place. I love watching content that inspires and encourages me. As a chronically ill and disabled woman, social media can sometimes be my only link to community, and what an incredibly supportive and loving community I have found on there. I love keeping up with my friends' lives, being inspired by what other people have made, and I follow many Christian accounts that give me important daily reminders to focus on God. Not to mention the fact that it has given me an accessible career that I can manage from home. I must admit, I wouldn't be without it.

But I will also readily say that it is problematic. Many studies have shown the huge rise in mental health problems, and the crisis we currently face has a lot to do with social media. The ability to see everything going on in the world all the time is overwhelming us, not to mention causing us all to constantly compare ourselves with others and become anxious that we aren't living our best lives. I am not a specialist in this area by any means, but it doesn't take long to do some research online and find out that social media can be very bad for us indeed.

Social media use can increase our levels of anxiety, depression, stress, comparison ... and all of these take us away from God. Lent is a great time to regain some control when it comes to social media. I have many friends who have given it up entirely for the whole seven weeks and found this a freeing experience. I personally have given it up for twenty-four hours every Sunday and felt the benefits.

Perhaps this Lent you might think about giving some of your social media time to God. Instead of thirty minutes of scrolling, you could add thirty minutes of prayer to your daily schedule. Instead of starting the day by checking your notifications, you could open your Bible. In the weeks leading up to Lent try to figure out when you usually scroll through social media and think about what else you might be able to do with that time.

Less tech

Another great option for Lent is to give up some screen time. That may be the same thing as giving up social media for you, or it might mean less TV or less phone time generally. Last year for Lent I gave my phone up for twenty-four hours every week on a Sunday. It was hard. The phone addiction is strong and turning it off each Saturday night and putting it in a drawer was quite painful.

But you know what? I managed it! I was able to go to church, go about my business and live my life without a phone. I was a little panicked that some major family disaster would happen while I was completely MIA, but it didn't and if it had they could have contacted my husband.

Not having my phone to check constantly on Sunday meant I was much more present. I was able to take in everything that was going on. We went for walks with the dog, and I didn't stop to take a hundred photos of the snowdrops (this was hard). Instead, I just enjoyed seeing them in real life. I learned that not everything has to be captured and kept. Some things can simply be enjoyed. It reminded me to stay present, to listen to what God had to say and to look at everything I had around me.

Whether it's a laptop, TV or phone, cutting down screen time is a great way to spend more time with God over Lent, and also with your friends and family. This one is definitely something you could decide to do as a household. Perhaps you could agree to one screenless night a week and instead play board games or do crafts. Maybe organise a weekly meet-up with friends, where phones are placed in a box at the door and no TV is allowed. Instead you just spend time together in a screen-free world.

Forty acts of kindness

Many of you will already have heard of this, but it is one of my favourite things that Christians do throughout Lent. The idea is that over the course of Lent you perform forty acts of kindness – one every day until Easter. These can be easy, like paying for the person behind you in the queue at the coffee shop, or they can require more sacrifice, such as offering to help repaint someone's living room. I've seen so many great acts of kindness throughout the years and I think to focus on sacrificial giving of both time and resources is a great thing to do during Lent. It is also something wonderful to get the whole family involved with.

One great way to do this is to come up with forty acts, write them on slips of paper and then pop them in a jar. Each day you pick one out and that is the act you will perform. This may not be the most accessible idea if you're chronically ill or disabled, so give yourself the flexibility you need to make it achievable. Remember that traditional Lent (beginning on Ash Wednesday) is actually forty-seven days long, so you have a few days' leeway.

There are loads of resources for this online, but here are some ideas to get you started:

- Buy a coffee for the person behind you in the queue.
- Cook a meal and drop it off to a neighbour or friend.
- Offer to babysit for a family at church.
- Take the time to compliment someone. It could be on their outfit or their singing voice – just make that person's day a little brighter.
- Take a friend out for dinner or a drink.
- Make something for someone – a beautiful handmade soap or a little pair of mittens.
- Donate to charity the money you would have spent this week on a coffee or something nice for yourself.
- Do a food shop for your local foodbank.
- Spend a few hours praying for people who are struggling right now.

- Take time to thank someone for something they did for you with a handwritten note.

Prayer for Lent

Lord, help us this Lent to focus on you; to look to the forty days you spent in the desert praying and fasting. Help us to want that level of devotion – to want to give this time to you, Lord. Give us courage to be generous with our time and resources. Help us to find you this season – to carve out time for you. Let us take this wonderful opportunity to grow in relationship with you. Lord, guide us to spend Lent in the way that will glorify you most as we prepare for that wonderful celebration of Easter. Amen.

SPRING

Bring me spring,
with its lukewarm sun,
with golden-headed daffodils nodding in biting winds,
and cherry blossom buds beginning to form.

Bring me spring,
with lambs and chicks and new mothers,
all learning and living and trying together.

Bring me spring,
with cleaning and busyness,
out with the old and in with the new,
seeds pushed into wet soil and green shoots growing.

Bring me spring,
with long days and shorter nights,
with sun streams glinting through curtains in the morning,
a reminder that even after the darkest of nights the light
   always returns.

Bring me spring,
with easter and eggs,
new hope and new life,
dreams to be dreamt and new starts to begin.

Bring me spring,
for spring brings me back again.

3
Gardening

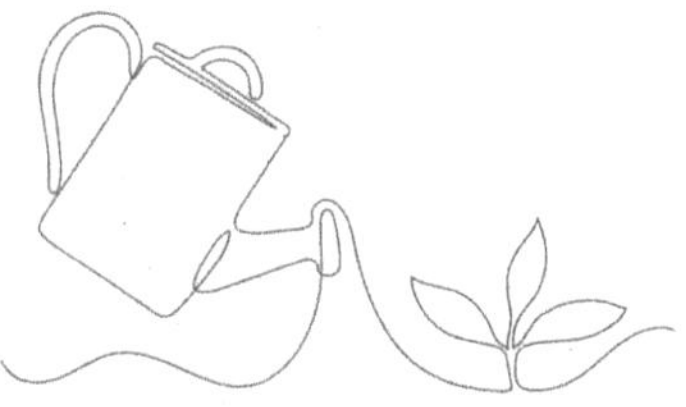

'Might I,' quavered Mary, 'might I have a bit of earth?'

In her eagerness she did not realize how queer the words would sound and that they were not the ones she had meant to say. Mr. Craven looked quite startled.

'Earth!' he repeated. 'What do you mean?'

'To plant seeds in – to make things grow – to see them come alive.'

Frances H. Burnett, *The Secret Garden*[6]

The LORD God took the man and put him in the Garden of Eden to work it and take care of it.
(Genesis 2:15)

I remember so clearly the first time I decided I wanted to plant something. I was nineteen years old and studying in Birmingham. I had taken myself off to my auntie Sarah's flat for dinner (a regular occurrence during that year!) and she suggested we watch something called *The Good Life*. It took one thrity-minute episode and I was hooked. I absolutely loved it.

For anyone who doesn't know, *The Good Life* is a 1970s British sit-com that follows the lives of Tom and Barbara Good. On his fortieth birthday Tom decides he needs to change his life. He no longer wants to work in the busy rat-race world of plastics design and instead decides to give it all up to become self-sufficient. But instead of selling their 1930s suburban home in Surrey, he and Barbara decide to turn it into a tiny smallholding.

They plough up the garden, get chickens, goats, pigs and even a cow at one point. It is hilarious and ridiculous, real comedy gold, and if you haven't seen it, I insist you go and watch an episode right now!

But this show had an incredible impact on me. It showed me a way of living that I had never thought about before. Growing up in the Wirral, life had been pretty suburban. Obviously people did grow veggies and there were allotments, but I didn't know anyone who had turned their garden into more than a big lawn with a few nice bushes and flowers. So even though *The Good Life* was a bit over the top and ridiculous in places, I was inspired by it. I wanted a garden to grow food in and keep chickens – maybe one day get a hive of bees. It started me on my journey towards what I like to call 'mini-homesteading'.

A beginning

Unfortunately, access to land in the UK for people of a younger generation is very hard to come by. Unless you have inherited it or have substantial financial means, the ability to buy land or a home with land is limited to the few. There is the option to move to rural parts of Wales or Scotland, where house prices are lower due to their rural locations, but then you often have to contend with a lack of work opportunities. For us, with my husband's work being firmly cemented in the South Midlands, we've had no choice but to stay put and deal with the often extremely high house prices. It has been hard. I am unable to take on an allotment due to my health. I need quick and easy access to my garden so that I can do twenty minutes here and there when the energy strikes me. So this is how I came to create my 'mini-homestead'.

I began in a small two-bedroom 1990s rented semi-detached house. It had a fairly good garden, even if it was very loud, positioned on the side of the A40. This was where I first got my hands dirty. It was the spring of 2020. Covid and lockdown had pushed us all into our gardens (if we were lucky enough to have them) and I decided I wanted to finally have a go at growing food. I'd been wanting to try it for seven years since first watching *The Good Life* and now was my time.

One morning I pulled out a packet of seeds and started to plant them up in takeaway tubs in our spare bedroom. With no greenhouse to speak of, the windowsill in the spare room was our best option, so it became my starting point. As I repeatedly placed my finger down into the soil to make small holes for the seeds, I felt a connection to the earth and creation. Before becoming ill, the natural world had been where I felt closest to God. I would go on walks through forests and along beaches, marvel at his creation and feel his presence with every step. But my mobility issues had made those walks difficult and painful. Feeling the soil with my bare fingers that day, I was reminded of the connection I'd once felt. A connection to the earth and its Creator.

Each day I watched in amazement as the tiny seeds began to grow into green shoots pushing their heads up through the soil – the same two little green leaves on every seedling heralding the beginning of new life. Each day they brought hope, and as I tended to them with water and turned them round on the windowsill to make sure they got enough sun, I felt God was with me.

Soon it was time to plant them outside. With some help from my husband, I got them all into pots on the patio of our rental property. As the days became sunnier and the plants grew stronger, I began to learn just how incredible creation was. Being very much a creative and someone who hadn't listened at all in school science lessons, I had no idea, until I started growing things, that every fruit begins as a flower and some are male and some female. I learned that each plant needs a bee to come along and take pollen from the male flower and move it to the female one for the fruit to grow. I couldn't believe just how intricate and magical creation was. This was true artistry, and I found myself marvelling at the Artist once more.

Soon I had courgettes and tomatoes to eat, all from those tiny seeds I'd planted in our bedroom back in March, along with raspberry and strawberry plants from the garden centre.

The mini-gardener

I felt, as I had all those years before, that this was part of the life God was calling me to. A slower life. Where food is grown at home, slowly and under my care. It was the slowest form of grocery shopping, but it just felt right.

When we moved to our little two-bedroom mid-terraced house in the Cotswolds, our garden was even smaller, but I knew we could make the most of it. That was when I started sharing about mini-homesteading on my social media. I knew I couldn't buy a smallholding. Even if I had the money, I wouldn't have the energy to run it. But instead, I could focus on what I could do right there and then with what I had.

Our garden is about 10 metres by 4 metres, and we've managed to grow rhubarb, apples, raspberries, strawberries, rosemary, mint, lemon balm, lavender, squash and pumpkins, courgettes, cucumbers, tomatoes, peppers, spinach, chard, mixed leaf salad, calendula and nasturtiums. And that's not to mention all the flowers: roses, peonies, hydrangeas, dahlias, tulips, daffodils, crocuses, alliums, Mexican orange blossom, ceanothus, clematis, sweet peas and hellebores. Quite a lot for such a small space. It just goes to show that you really don't need a large garden to grow your own food. There are tons of books (see suggestions on the Resources page), YouTube videos and articles about growing – no matter what your outdoor space looks like. From balconies to terraced gardens to allotments, there's always room to grow somewhere.

Even if you have no outdoor space at all, you can still grow inside. A few years ago, my good friend Harry decided to give it a go. As every good gardener does, I had planted up more seeds for my chilli plants than I needed, just in case some didn't come through, so I had plenty to spare. He took a few home and grew them on the windowsill of his flat. By the end of the summer, he had more big, ripe, red chillies than he knew what to do with! And he's officially been bitten by the growing bug. Now his flat in London is so full of beautiful, well-tended house plants, it would rival a Kew Gardens greenhouse.

Growing is a revolutionary act

In a time when land is scarce and convenience is king, growing your own food, flowers and herbs is a revolutionary act. It's taking back a bit of power – taking control and becoming just a little more self-sufficient, even if all you've grown is a few windowsill chillies like Harry. It's also a wonderful way to connect with our Creator. For me there is nothing like an afternoon with my hands in the dirt, pushing seeds into soil, tending to new shoots or pruning aging trees to help remind me that God is all around us. He is making everything new every day through his creation and he encourages us to be a part of that.

It wasn't just a coincidence that we were born into a garden and asked to tend it. This is a place to find peace, to stay in the present moment, to accept our lack of control and give it all to our Creator. We can give our plants the best start in life – a lovely warm windowsill or greenhouse, lots of water and rich compost – but at the end of the day we simply have to be patient and hope for the best, and I think that is a wonderful lesson for us to learn in a world of immediacy and instant gratification.

Start your growing journey this year. I promise you won't regret it!

Where to begin

Okay, so now I have successfully convinced you to don the gardening gloves and turn into your best version of Monty Don, you're probably thinking, 'Where on earth do I start?'

If you're reading this book at the beginning of the year or in the springtime, then you're in luck! You can begin growing food and flowers right now! If, however, it's currently November and all a bit cold and dreary outside, you might want to shelve the gardening gloves for a few months when it comes to food. You can still, however, pop in a few bulbs to brighten up the early spring months. Take a look below for advice on where to begin, and start by gathering together the following equipment:

- Pots or raised beds
- Peat-free compost
- Trowel
- Fork
- Seed trays
- Seedling labels
- Gardening gloves
- Watering can

Spring and summer

The best time to start growing in the UK is around March. This is the point at which you can start off some seeds. But before you rush to the garden centre, you need to have a think about your available space.

Where to grow

Whether you have a balcony or two acres of garden, the most important thing to learn is where the sun rises and sets. Basically, are you north facing or south facing? This will determine the kind of plants you can grow. If you're north facing, you will have to choose plants that enjoy being in shade most of the day and thrive in cooler temperatures. If you're south facing, you will need plants that love the sunshine, as they will be getting a lot of it. If you're somewhere in the middle, then try to track just how much sun the various parts of your space get throughout the day. Try to count the hours and this will give you a good idea of what you can plant there.

The next thing to decide is whether you will grow your plants in pots, raised beds or the ground. If you're in a rental or have a balcony, you might decide that pots are the way to go. If, like me, you have a flat garden to work with, you could build some raised beds. You might even already have beds in your garden that you can use. If you have a small space, I suggest you look into growing vertically. We have two espalier apple trees in our small garden that take up minimal space because they grow flat against the fence. Over the last few years, we've managed to get a good crop of apples from these, and every year we get more and more. Gardening well isn't just about the space you have available; it's also about how you use that space.

What to grow

Next, you'll need to work out what you would like to grow. Is it food you're interested in, or flowers? Perhaps a bit of both? What flowers do you like? What food do you like? It's important you grow what you actually care about, or you'll lose interest and all the work you've put in will be for nothing. Rocket is one of the easiest things to grow in pretty much any garden, but I cannot stand the taste, so I've never grown it. Choose things you're excited about.

Here are some suggestions you might like to try as a beginner.

Food

Raspberries – these are so easy to grow in pots or in a small space. If you buy autumn-fruiting raspberries you can sometimes get a double crop – one in the summer and one in the autumn. You can also pop raspberries into a bed and just leave them to do their thing, simply making sure they have enough water every so often. They're my favourite low-maintenance food plants to grow. Plant up in March for fruit in summer/autumn.

Spinach/chard/rocket/speedy salad mix – I've grouped these together as they are all leafy greens that are super-easy to grow. You need a bit more room for spinach and chard, but they are great cut-and-come-again plants, so give you a lot of food for your effort. Rocket and speedy salad mix are wonderful for small, shallow beds or even window boxes. You just sprinkle the seeds over the soil and keep well watered. You will get so many lovely leaves for your summer table, and nothing tastes fresher than homegrown salad! Plant up under cover in a greenhouse or inside in March, then plant out in April once the chance of frost has gone.

Courgettes – These are relatively easy to grow, but if you are growing them in pots they will need to be fairly large and deep. Courgettes are very prolific, so will keep giving you fruit all summer long. They are such a versatile food. From salads, to paellas to fritters and even lemon and courgette cake, they make such a tasty addition to your kitchen garden. Plant up seeds under cover in a greenhouse or inside in April, or plant seeds straight out in May once the chance of frost has gone.

Strawberries – These are very easy to grow and can be grown in small spaces, such as window boxes or hanging baskets. They need to be well protected from birds as soon as they begin to go red and must be kept well watered, but otherwise they aren't much work at all and that taste of the first summer strawberry from the garden is so sweet. Plant up strawberry plants in March/April using a strawberry planter, hanging basket or any container that is at least 15 centimetres deep.

Rhubarb – If you have a garden bed already and are planning to stay in your home for a while, I would recommend growing some rhubarb. You can't harvest it for the first couple of years while you're waiting for the plant to establish, but then you'll get sticks and sticks of the stuff. It is a very forgiving plant. We named ours Lazarus, because every time we thought we'd killed it, it would return! Plant rhubarb crowns in March/April, but remember not to harvest for a couple of years until a healthy plant has grown.

Flowers

Annuals – If you're in the throes of spring, a great place to start with flowers is annuals. These are seeds you sow every year as they only grow for one year. Once they go over, they are finished. They will go to seed and, if left, nature can take its course, but I prefer to give nature a helping hand and collect the seed heads and resprinkle them the following year. Some annuals to try are zinnia, ami majus, nigella and cosmos. These little flowers are not hardy, so you will have to wait until late March if growing in a greenhouse or late May when all fear of frost has passed to sprinkle directly into the beds. I've had a lot of success just sprinkling them into beds in late May, but it does mean your flower crop will come later.

Shrubs – If you'd like a very easy way to grow flowers that requires very little effort and you have space for pots or a flower bed, I recommend you get yourself some shrubs. These are plants which, if taken care of, will flower year after year. You can buy them in all different sizes from the garden centre, although the larger ones can be very costly. This is how we began our flower bed, filling it with shrubs that after a few years have really taken off and bring us beautiful flowers each summer. Some of my favourites are ceanothus, Mexican orange blossom, roses and miniature lilac.

Perennials – These are plants that grow back year after year. Some easy flowers to try are peonies, climbers such as clematis and jasmine, and hydrangeas.

Autumn and winter

There aren't a lot of jobs to do in the garden during the autumn and winter seasons. It's a great time to do some tidying and sorting, pruning of fruit trees and diving into seed catalogues, looking forward to the spring season.

Growing in the colder months

There are some things that can be grown this time of year for the more seasoned gardener, but if you're new to it I'd suggest trying a bit of spinach or kale. These are easy to plant up in the late summer, when it's still warm enough to get your seedlings going, and they will keep giving you fresh green leaves throughout the colder months. And you can grow flowers …

October to December is the perfect time to plant some bulbs into pots or garden beds and, trust me, come the dark, cold February days you'll be pleased you did. There is nothing better than seeing those first green shoots of a bulb poking up through the hard frozen soil during Lent to remind you of the hope we have in Jesus. I would suggest starting with daffodils and tulips. You'll need some good pots to withstand the frozen winter, or a garden bed. The back of the bulb packet will tell you how deep to bury them, but a good rule of thumb is normally two times the size of the bulb itself, so if the bulb is 5 centimetres you'd make a 10-centimetre hole for it. Bulbs are easy. You essentially just bury them and leave them, but the one thing you need to remember is not to let them touch. They can be very close in the soil, but not touching.

Keep it wild

As humans, we have a selfish trait of assuming the world is just for us. We have become very bad at sharing it with the rest of God's beautiful creation and sadly some irreparable damage has been done. But not all is lost. We can still make a huge difference to the planet as a whole simply by the way we choose to garden.

Choosing to garden consciously, with wildlife in mind, is a great way to make a difference in your local area. You may be thinking, 'What difference can one small garden make?' but the truth is, if we all tried to garden consciously, we could change an entire neighbourhood or even country. Change can start small, with you and your own back garden. Here are some things to think about when gardening:

Peat free

If you don't have space to make your own compost (most of us don't!), you will need to buy some. Therefore, it is important that you choose the best option. Peat-free compost is readily available. Peat is a soft organic material that works as a carbon sink, so when it is extracted from the ground, it causes more carbon to be released into the environment. Try to buy the best compost you can afford – organic, responsibly sourced and peat free.

Organic

Growing can be a tricky business, with fly infestations, caterpillars munching all your seedlings, blight, mould, rot – and that is to name just a few. As you watch all your hard work begin to go to waste thanks to the uncontrollable wet weather (especially with climate change these days), it can be tempting to go to the garden centre and pick up a simple spray that will fix the issue. But one of the best ways we can help our garden and our planet to thrive is to go organic. Pests such as greenfly, blackfly, caterpillars and slugs are a great source of food for many wildlife, so it is important we allow them into our gardens. But when it gets a little out of control, try to choose greener methods of pest control, such as homemade chilli and garlic sprays, eggshells, copper rings and gravel. There is a wealth of knowledge out there on natural organic gardening, so check out some of the books on the Resources page for more information.

A home for wildlife

Creating a welcoming environment for wildlife is a great way to make a difference in your garden space. You can do this in lots of ways, but here are a few ideas to get you started:

- Place bird feeders around your garden, filled with wild bird seed. Make sure you regularly clean these to help stop the spread of avian disease. You can also put out bird baths, which are essential for thirsty birds, bees and other wildlife during the hotter months.
- Leave a small gap in your fence to allow hedgehogs in and out. Hedgehogs are great at eating slugs, so they are wonderful to have in your garden when it comes to pest control.
- Create a wildlife pond. This can be as big or as small as you like. You could use an old sink or a trug to create a space for wildlife such as newts, frogs and dragonflies to drink from. Just make sure you put

steps inside your container, using stones or rocks, so anything that falls in can easily get out.

- Don't cut the grass too much. Leave it longer than you usually would, or better still leave a whole patch nice and long. We have always had a wild patch in the garden, left to do its own thing. This makes a good home for any wildlife that needs it. We tend to cut it once a year at the end of summer.
- Choose plants that are good for the bees. I am very partial to a triple-headed peony, tulip or daffodil, but these are very hard for bees to get inside to collect pollen. I always make sure I have a range of plants that I know will be a good food source for bees.

Of course you want to protect your harvest from pests and get the best yield you can, but this is their home too and I think a more relaxed approach to growing is much healthier. I am happy to share some of my homegrown produce with the wildlife and accept that not all the strawberries and raspberries will make it. The birds deserve some too! If blackfly moves in on a stem of my runner beans, I will sacrifice the stem and accept that I have enough on the rest of the plant. I'm sure many gardeners would frown at this, but I find it to be a healthier and easier mindset.

Getting started as a gardener can feel very overwhelming. I remember that at the beginning I read so many books telling me thousands of different things and I didn't understand half of it. But after just four years of gardening, I'm starting to know the difference between my perennial and my annual. It takes time, practice and to be honest quite a lot of good luck. You can do everything right, but at the end of the day you're always at the mercy of the weather. That is the beauty of gardening. It is something that cannot be controlled, the outcome can never be certain, and you learn so much about slowing down and staying present as you garden.

There is something truly beautiful about tending a garden. It intrinsically links us to our Creator. It captures something innate and deep inside of us, reminding us of the job we were first given when God placed us on this earth. If you're feeling stressed and burnt out, digging your hands deep into the earth will help ground you and bring you back to the one who helps make sense of it all.

Note: I could have written an entire gardening manual with the amount I wish to share, but there are people who have already done this, and a lot better than I ever could! I hope this chapter has piqued your interest in gardening, but for some real solid advice on where to start and how to grow plants, please check out the Resources page, where I share a number of books that have helped me greatly on my gardening journey.

Seasonal celebrations: Easter

On the first day of the week, very early in the morning, the women took the spices they had prepared and went to the tomb. They found the stone rolled away from the tomb, but when they entered, they did not find the body of the Lord Jesus. While they were wondering about this, suddenly two men in clothes that gleamed like lightning stood beside them. In their fright the women bowed down with their faces to the ground, but the men said to them, 'Why do you look for the living among the dead? He is not here; he has risen! Remember how he told you, while he was still with you in Galilee: "The Son of Man must be delivered over to the hands of sinners, be crucified and on the third day be raised again."' Then they remembered his words.

When they came back from the tomb, they told all these things to the Eleven and to all the others. It was Mary Magdalene, Joanna, Mary the mother of James, and the others with them who told this to the apostles. But they did not believe the women, because their words seemed to them like nonsense. Peter, however, got up and ran to the tomb. Bending over, he saw the strips of linen lying by themselves, and he went away, wondering to himself what had happened.

(Luke 24:1–12)

Easter is the biggest celebration in the Christian calendar. It is the day we celebrate what our faith is truly about: that Jesus died for us and rose again so that we might all have eternal life with him. The days leading up to Easter are a beautiful time of reflection with a joyous and full celebration at the end. But like many Christian festivals in the UK, Easter has sadly lost a lot of its meaning in the wider world.

I grew up with a Christian mum. She was the first person to take me to church and introduce me to my faith. She made sure Easter was about Jesus and not just chocolate. I can still remember the first time I realised Easter looked very different for other people. I was a teen watching a famous YouTuber, and she described Easter as 'a celebration of chocolate'. I remember being quite shocked. This most important event, which had always been one of the busiest times of the year in our church, was reduced to eating as much chocolate as you could?

As an adult now I realise she didn't know any better. She hadn't been shown an alternative to the celebration and probably wasn't aware of how offensive her comment was to Christians. If you look around at Easter celebrations today, that is pretty much what you see. We now find creme eggs going out on the shelves on Boxing Day, speeding away from Christmas and finding the next money-maker as soon as possible. Easter seems to hit in a whirlwind of brightly covered chocolate eggs that are everywhere for months. People are frenzied in the weeks leading up to Easter, buying egg after egg after egg and stashing them away to gorge on over the weekend.

This is a pretty shoddy show for an occasion that celebrates the risen Lord Jesus! I want to propose something different this year. I want us to slow down, remember the 'reason for the season' (I know this phrase is normally used at Christmas, but it works for Easter too!) and maybe get as excited about Easter celebrations as we do Christmas. There may be a lot less in the way of presents for Easter, but Jesus' sacrifice is the greatest gift of all, and although this should be something we keep in our hearts all year round, Easter is a great time to remind ourselves of the truth of God's promise. It is also a wonderful time to share this gift with others.

So how about it? Shall we try a slow and beautiful Easter celebration together this year?

Holy Week

Holy Week was a busy time for my church as a child. There were so many exciting events going on. It often falls within the Easter break, which allows parents and children to really enjoy the celebration together. If you aren't a parent and/or you're working during this time, there are still lots of ways you can enjoy this week.

Palm Sunday

This is one of my favourite Sundays of the year! I have the fondest memories of handmade palm crosses being given out, and parading around the church yard shouting, 'Hosanna in the highest!' It was a great opportunity for the kids of the church to really get involved and catch the excitement of a life following Jesus. I remember one year they even hired a donkey to walk around the church yard with us!

I know that not every church will be able to do this. Indeed, the churches my husband and I have attended as adults have mostly gathered in school or town halls and I think we'd get into rather a lot of trouble if we brought a donkey inside! We have, however, always found ways to celebrate this time of year with much branch waving (not normally palm leaves, being based in the Cotswolds, but they work!) and shouting hosanna. If your church doesn't do this, I really recommend you speak to the leadership and try to encourage a joyful celebration on Palm Sunday with hymns and praises.

But we can also celebrate at home. Making palm crosses is a fun activity for all the family, and I encourage you to have a go at this. You can order supplies online.

In Norway, Palm Sunday is traditionally the time when the house is decorated for Easter, and I think this is a great way to start the celebrations. Here are some ideas for decorations.

Easter tree

The Easter tree originated in Germany and Austria, but is now a tradition many Christians all over the world have adopted. It is such an easy but effective decoration, and it makes a fun crafting session on Palm Sunday. All you need is a large branch with lots of small branches coming off it. I find that one of the prettiest to use is a blossom branch from a fruit tree. Try to find one with buds just starting to open. The indoor warmth will bring the flowers out over the week and by Easter you will have a beautiful floral Easter tree. (Remember to collect your branch responsibly, being sympathetic to nature and making sure you have permission to take it.)

Next you need your eggs. Eggs are a symbol of new life, the new life we have in Jesus, so I love to decorate the house with them at this time of year. There are so many ways to do this. Traditionally you would decorate real eggs, piercing them with small holes and sucking out the raw egg so that you are left with an empty shell. You can then paint, dye or even stick dried flowers to them.

Another option is to buy plain wooden or ceramic eggs and decorate them to use for years to come. I have a collection of beautiful hand-painted wooden eggs that I bought from a Fairtrade shop, and I love to bring these out each year.

A final option is to knit, sew or crochet some eggs that again can be used year on year. Whatever you do, remember that Easter is about joy and new life. It is a time for bright pastel colours that remind us of fresh starts and spring, so get out those pinks, blues, greens and yellows!

Pace eggs

The following is a tutorial on pace eggs, and how to dye them, by my mother-in-law, Ruth Bearn:

> The word 'pace' is derived from the Latin word *pascha*, meaning Easter. Pace eggs bring back happy childhood memories for me, of wandering the bit of moorland on our farm collecting bright yellow whins (the flowers from gorse bushes) and trying not to get too prickled by the thorny bushes. We would then all sit round the farmhouse kitchen table and begin to make our pace eggs. This was a process of dyeing the eggs with the flowers and onion skins. We would experiment with daffodil leaves, ferns and other flowers to see what made pretty patterns against the dark red of the onion skins. We wrapped the daffodil leaves round to try to create a cross or ribbon around the egg. I remember whins and daffodils working best, giving bright yellow patterns.
>
> Once wrapped in the onion skins and newspaper, they would be carefully packed into a pan and boiled. I was always impatient for them to boil then cool enough to unwrap and reveal the pretty patterns on the eggs. We would rub butter on them while they were still warm to make them shine, and my mum used to say it helped them last longer too. They would then be arranged in a bowl and set in pride of place on the sideboard, but not of course before arguing with my brothers as to whose was the best! I always thought they tasted far better than ordinary hard-boiled eggs.
>
> In some places people roll the eggs down a hill on Easter Day to represent the stone being rolled away from Jesus' tomb.

Ingredients and equipment

- 12 white or pale eggs
- Whins (gorse flowers) or other soft foliage
- Brown onion skins, as whole as possible
- Newspaper and thread
- Kitchen roll
- Butter

Method

1. Dampen the outside of the eggs to help keep the flowers or leaves in place. Arrange your petals and leaves in the design you want.
2. Wrap the eggs tightly in the onion skins until no patches of eggshell can be seen.
3. Carefully wrap in newspaper, then tie with thread to keep in place. If you don't have newspaper you could try tightly wrapping in foil.
4. Pack the wrapped eggs tightly into a pan so they don't move when boiling.
5. Cover with water, bring to the boil, then simmer for 15 minutes.
6. Remove from heat and allow to cool.
7. When cool enough to handle, carefully peel the paper and onion skins off the eggs.
8. While still warm, rub the eggs with butter using a bit of kitchen roll.
9. Arrange in a bowl and display on your Easter table.

Maundy Thursday and Good Friday

There are many traditions in the Church relating to Maundy Thursday, from washing feet (reflecting Jesus washing the feet of his disciples) to stripping altars, taking communion and wearing black clothing. Growing up, Maundy Thursday and Good Friday was the time when the Mothers' Union would create their beautiful Easter garden. This was a miniature garden that was displayed in the church over the Easter weekend. It would vary from year to year, but it always had a tomb with a stone in front of it and a row of three crosses. On Easter Day the stone would be rolled away in the early morning before church, and we children used to love coming in to see the open tomb.

Back home we would create our own miniature Easter garden, and it's a tradition I have enjoyed taking into adulthood. It's something the whole family can get involved in, but it's also an opportunity to have a relaxing afternoon by yourself, meditating on the Easter story and marvelling at God's beautiful creation.

Easter garden tutorial

Equipment

- A tray of some sort (we normally use a seed tray with deep sides). This will be filled with soil, so do choose something you aren't too precious about!
- Soil or compost
- Secateurs
- Rocks or pebbles
- Sticks
- Flowers and small branches from the garden
- White tissue paper
- Optional: tin foil, moss, palm crosses

Method

1. Fill the tray with soil.
2. Forage in the garden or neighbourhood (make sure you have permission) for flowers, leaves, branches – anything that takes your fancy.
3. Place your stones in a tomb shape. I often choose three to create a sort of pyramid with an opening, then I place a fourth in front, ready to be rolled away on Easter Day. You can place some white tissue paper or cloth, to represent Jesus' grave clothes, inside your mini-tomb ready for Easter Day!
4. Decorate your garden with flowers, and branches to look like trees. In the past I have made tiny gravel paths and created a pond from some tin foil and 'floated' a flower in it.
5. You can use palm crosses, or perhaps tie sticks together to form three crosses, which can be placed in one corner of the garden to represent Jesus and the two men he was crucified with.
6. Don't forget to roll the stone away on Easter morning!

Easter Day

It is estimated that more than 4,000 tonnes of plastic waste are produced at Easter. And in the UK more than £960 million is spent on food and drink for the celebration. I love a chance to celebrate as much as the next person, but as Christians I think we have a responsibility to slow down our consumption and remember what is important. We have the opportunity to do Easter gifting, decorating and eating differently. Here are some ways to be a little more sustainable this Easter:

- Decorate with natural ornaments or make reusable decorations that you bring out year after year (see above).
- Buy fewer eggs! We don't all need seven chocolate eggs this year. Why not buy one per person and buy better, choosing Fairtrade and plastic free.
- Cut down your chocolate egg consumption even further by creating a sharing basket of mini-eggs. Fill a small basket with shredded brown paper, then pop in lots of Fairtrade chocolate eggs for the family to dip into over the Sunday. You could even add a handmade chick or two.
- Choose local, organic farm food for your Easter Day feast. And if you can't find anything local, see what you can order in the UK. Our personal favourite place to order from is Riverford Organic.
- Make your own eggs and treats. You can buy silicone chocolate moulds to be used again and again, allowing you to create delicious treats exactly to your taste every year. You can place these in little baskets without wrapping, which saves on the plastic and foil waste.

Nana's chocolate flake cake (with added chocolate eggs)

This is a favourite recipe in my family – one that has been passed down from my nana to my mum, to her children, and now my mum is Nana and making it with her grandchildren. It is a simple chocolate sponge, and I have added some extra eggs to make it perfect for an Easter Day treat.

Ingredients

- 300 g butter, plus a little extra for greasing
- 200 g caster sugar
- 4 medium sized eggs
- 200 g self-raising flour
- 4–6 tbsp cocoa powder
- 200 g icing sugar
- 200 g milk chocolate
- 2 chocolate flakes (the large ones)
- 1 bag mini chocolate eggs

Method

1. Preheat your oven to 200°C/180°C fan/gas 6.
2. Grease two 16-cm cake tins with butter and set aside.
3. Take 200 g of the softened butter and place in a mixer or bowl. Add in the caster sugar and mix well.
4. Add the eggs, one at a time, until combined.
5. Add the flour, a quarter at a time, mixing it in well.
6. Mix in the cocoa powder a tablespoon at a time.
7. Test the mixture to see if it tastes chocolatey enough for you. If not, add more cocoa powder.
8. Split the mix evenly between the cake tins and place in the oven for 20–25 minutes. It is sometimes hard to tell

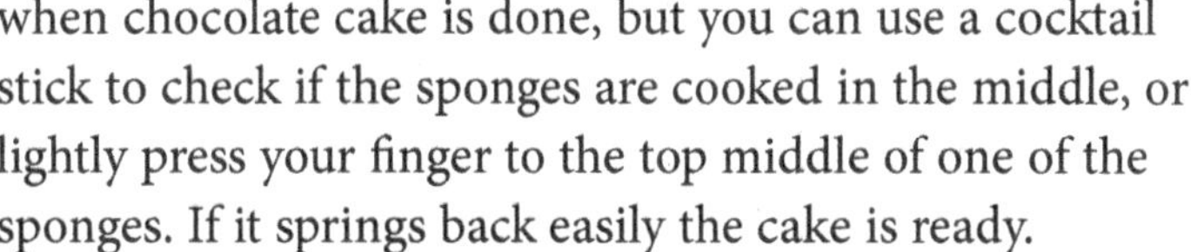

when chocolate cake is done, but you can use a cocktail stick to check if the sponges are cooked in the middle, or lightly press your finger to the top middle of one of the sponges. If it springs back easily the cake is ready.

9 Leave to cool completely.

10 Place 100 g softened butter into your mixer or bowl (if using a bowl, you will need an electric hand-held whisk). Beat for five minutes until the butter is pale and fluffy.

11 Add in the icing sugar a little at a time, continuing to mix thoroughly.

12 Once all the icing sugar is combined, add in 1 tbsp of cocoa powder and mix.

13 Do a taste test of the butter cream. If it tastes chocolatey enough for you, it's ready. If not, keep adding cocoa powder until it is right.

14 Once the sponges have cooled, place one on a plate (this will be your serving plate). Using a palette knife or flat knife, spread buttercream across the sponge until you have an even layer. Place the other sponge on top.

15 Break up the chocolate and melt in a bain-marie or in the microwave, remembering to check it regularly so it doesn't burn. Once melted, leave to cool for a couple of minutes before pouring on top of your cake. Smooth across the top and allow it to set for 5–10 minutes.

16 Once the chocolate has cooled a little but is still sticky, crumble your flakes on top. Add your mini-eggs and leave the top to set completely (this will take a few hours).

17 Serve up your Easter flake cake and enjoy!

4
Clothes

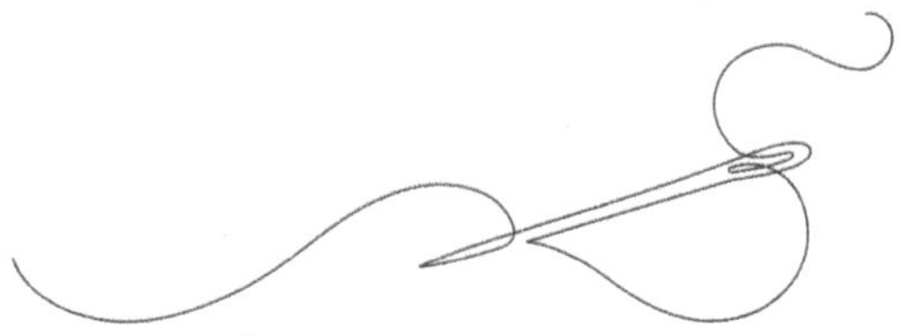

> Slow clothing is a philosophy. It is a way of thinking about, choosing, wearing and caring for clothes to ensure they bring meaning, value and joy to every day.
> (Jane Milburn)[7]

> Therefore, as God's chosen people, holy and dearly loved, clothe yourselves with compassion, kindness, humility, gentleness and patience.
> (Colossians 3:12)

I've always loved fashion ever since I was little. I don't mean trends and big brands; I'm talking about style. To me clothes are a great way to express who you are and how you're feeling. I started my first fashion blog when I was seventeen as a way to challenge myself to style fun and interesting outfits within the parameters of the sixth-form office-wear dress code. As you can imagine, I did get told off quite a few times when I pushed the boundaries a little too far, but I enjoyed that sense of self-expression that came with trying new ways of dressing.

Later, in my early twenties, I began to hear about the horrifying effects of the fashion industry on the planet and its people (more on that later), and I started to learn about something called 'slow fashion'. The slow fashion movement is all about slowing down our rate of consumption, choosing high-quality clothes and styles that will stand the test of time, and putting the planet and people above trends. To me as a new Christian, this all made plain sense, and I was soon writing my blog from the perspective of a newbie trying her best to dress sustainably.

When I became unwell in my mid-twenties, fashion went out of the window. My body changed hugely, and I had no control over it. I could no longer fit into any of the clothes I had carefully bought and curated over years, and I found it very difficult. I was also struggling to leave the house and in an awful lot of pain, so a lot of my wardrobe wasn't working for me anyway.

The loss of my personal style was tangible evidence of how I was feeling inside. I was in survival mode – any clothes that were vaguely comfortable and okay would do. I punished myself for putting on weight, despite it being very much out of my control, and I refused to buy any new clothes that actually fit. When I got desperate due to having nothing to wear, I would buy one frumpy, oversized garment just to get me through, because soon I would be better and would get my old body back! It was a miserable time, and I had forgotten the most important thing of all. Despite illness, despite weight gain, despite my changing body, I was a still a child of God – loved by the King and beautiful no matter what.

In 2022 I decided to make a change. I had been knitting for a while by then, but mostly baby garments for friends. For years I had wanted to learn to sew my own dresses and knit matching cardigans, but I just hadn't had enough energy. Moving house gave us the chance to set up a little sewing space for me. It was somewhere I was able to sit for a short time each day and sew. I didn't have to use my precious energy to get all the sewing equipment out and set it up each time I wanted to sew. Instead, it was all waiting for me and I simply had to sit down at the machine and pick up where I left off. Some days I would sew for just twenty minutes and others a full hour. I never went over an hour and a half though, to protect my health and energy, but being at the machine every day I began to find myself again.

My first few dresses weren't the best. I made one in a William Morris fabric, which was lovely but sadly far too tight across my bust. I had to learn about fit and ease and different fabrics. It was a lot at first, but slowly and surely I began to make myself a wardrobe that fitted, showed off my personal style, had a lower impact on the planet and, most importantly, worked around my chronic illnesses.

Over the last few years of sewing, comfy but pretty dresses have become my thing. I have a whole wardrobe of them, and I love them. They give me so much confidence and I love the slow process of making them. I try to choose deadstock (see page 83) or thrifted fabrics and if I end up making something that isn't quite right, I will always try to make something else from it so that nothing is wasted. It's been an amazing few years and I have loved sharing it all online. It's led to some fantastic experiences, such as appearing on Channel 4's *Kirstie's Handmade Christmas* with my own knitted design, and walking the catwalk at the Stitch Festival in London in a sparkling black floor-length gown I made for a black-tie event.

You may not care too much about clothes or fashion and that is totally okay. Everyone has their thing and maybe this isn't yours. But I hope this chapter will help to inspire and encourage you that even if clothes aren't your focus, you can still make a huge difference with what you wear. If, like me, you love to express yourself through what you wear but have often felt judged or misunderstood by the Christian community, I hope this chapter will encourage you to wear your personal style with pride. And if you need to dress a certain way due to a disability or illness, I hope you too will be inspired to make a change for yourself and the planet with your wardrobe. We all wear clothes, so this chapter has something for everyone, and I hope you will enjoy learning more about slowing your wardrobe down and making it work for you.

The problem with fashion

It is said that if we stopped producing clothes right now, we would still have enough clothes on the planet to clothe the next seven generations. That is insane. Can you even get your head around that? We are producing clothes at the most ridiculous rate, and it is only getting worse. We buy more clothes per person in the UK than any other country in Europe. We are addicted to buying clothes and it needs to stop.

Sadly, clothes these days are made to be disposable. They are made cheaply and quickly, mostly abroad if you live in the UK, in factories where people are not paid properly or treated in a fair way. Fast fashion is killing our planet and harming thousands of people all over the world. Garment workers are forced to work ridiculous hours in terrible conditions. Rivers and essential water supplies are filled with dangerous toxic chemical waste from factories, and people are forced against their will to pick cotton for our clothes. And this is just a small scratch on the surface of the effects of the fashion industry. I could write an entire book on the environmental and ethical effects resulting from the clothes we wear. But instead, I encourage you to go away and read about it for yourself. I have suggested some helpful and informative books and documentaries on the Resources page.

As Christians who profess to love our neighbours as ourselves, I cannot in all consciousness think it is okay to buy into this. Is it not our duty as children of God to love our neighbours wherever they may be? Whether it is right next door or in a cotton field in Uzbekistan or a garment factory in Bangladesh? We have a duty as God's people to care about this – to care about how the people making our clothes are being treated. We also have a responsibility to steward the earth well; to take care of God's creation and not buy clothes that hurt it.

Power in the pound

Every time we spend money we are making a choice. We may not realise it, but we are voting for the kind of world we want. We often think about how we conduct ourselves in the world – the way we speak to people, what our body language is telling others. As Christians this is important. We are called to love and show God's love wherever we are. And that includes what we do with our money. Yes, generous giving is important, but is it not a little hypocritical to be giving to charities working in countries that are directly affected by the climate crisis and then buying all our clothing from a fast-fashion brand that directly affects the climate?

I have met a lot of Christians in my time who aren't into clothes. They choose to spend as little money and time on their wardrobe as possible. And this is fine to a degree. Spending little money on our clothes by buying them at fast-fashion outlets may appear less materialistic, but it has a direct and significantly harmful effect on our planet. There is a better way to do it, whether we care about fashion or not.

When it comes to buying clothes, we have a choice. We can make a positive difference or a negative difference. It doesn't matter if we're looking for a snazzy outfit to wear to the next church ceilidh or just something that will do for every day. What we buy and how we buy our clothes matters. So how can we do it better?

Slow your wardrobe down

The first thing to do when moving towards a more sustainable wardrobe is to slow your wardrobe down. Just stop buying clothes and wear the ones you've already got. It is as simple as that. Most of us in the UK have a ridiculous amount of clothes. Be honest with yourself. If you stopped shopping for clothes for the next five years could you get by? I think most of us would answer yes. We have plenty of clothes, so the first step is to simply stop buying any new ones for a bit. And if you struggle to stop, I suggest not even looking. Don't go shopping. Don't check out the online stores, and unsubscribe from all those shopping emails. Remember to unfollow on social media as well! Having a detox from the constant barrage of marketing that comes our way telling us how much we desperately need shiny new things all the time can be life changing. These days I only shop when I actually need or want something. I rarely mindlessly peruse. And, believe me, it is liberating!

The big sort out

Okay, so now you've stopped buying clothes for a little while it's time to sort out what is actually in your wardrobe. Give yourself a whole day to sort through all the clothes you own – heck, why not a whole weekend (I know I would need it). Start creating separate piles: clothes you want to keep; clothes that need a bit of TLC and maybe some mending, but would be all right if you fixed them up; clothes to donate or sell. Then there will be a small pile of clothes that need to go to textile waste. I bet you'll find some items you had forgotten about or weren't expecting. It can be a really helpful way to find more clothes to wear without spending a single penny.

Once you've got your piles sorted, you can start putting the 'clothes to keep' pile away. This is the time to go full on Marie Kondo here. I like to carefully order my clothes so they are easy to see and find, which means I know exactly what I've got and I avoid those 'I've got so many clothes but nothing to wear' moments. I would also highly recommend sorting your clothes into autumn/winter and spring/summer. I keep half my wardrobe in storage under the bed and swap it over every six months. It means less chaos and I can actually see the clothes I have available to wear.

Identify gaps

Once you've sorted through all your clothes and you've been wearing them, you may discover you could do with a new jacket or pair of boots for winter. Take your time with this. Identify the gaps in your wardrobe by waiting it out a little to see if these are items you really need. Don't immediately make your way to the shops or check online and get tempted by pretty, shiny new things. Make sure they are actually items you will use and wear. If they are, then go ahead, but you might find there's one more season in those old boots.

Find your personal style

Before you do any shopping, you need to figure out your personal style. I am not talking trends here. Trends drive fast fashion and are not something to aspire to or follow. Finding our personal style is a much more unique and sustainable way to dress.

I've been honing my own sense of style for years now. I like classic, timeless shapes but with feminine and vintage details, and quite a lot of pattern and colour. Knowing this helps me to accurately assess whether I should bring a new garment into my wardrobe. If I see something that is a bit out there and not my usual style, I think very hard about whether it will get enough wear to justify a place in my wardrobe. I think about what it will go with, how I will wear it and if it will stand the test of time. This also means that when I see something in my usual style, I can assess whether it is too similar to an item I already own and if there is an actual need for it. It allows me to see immediately how it will work in my wardrobe.

It can be hard to find your personal style, but I would suggest you start with keeping a folder of outfits you like from social media. I follow a few fashion Instagrammers and I get a lot of inspiration from their outfits. Often, they simply inspire me to style what I already have in a different way.

I also love to keep a Pinterest board and normally take some time each season to put together a style board for the season. This helps me to think about new and fun ways to style the clothes I already have and to see any gaps there might be in my wardrobe. I recently did this for autumn/winter and it allowed me to see that if I bought a second-hand tweed jacket to go with the dresses I already had, I could style them in a slightly more mature way than I had done in past years. I ended up buying a gorgeous second-hand tweed jacket from Vinted that will stay in my wardrobe for years!

Sustainable shopping

Now that you've stopped buying unnecessarily, found your personal style and started styling your current clothes in a different way, you're probably wondering what to do when you do need something new. Below are my top tips for buying second-hand and sustainable fashion.

Buying second-hand

Write a list

As much as we try to slow things down, the reality is that sometimes there will be items we need quickly (when you run out of toothpaste or deodorant, you need a trip to the shops!). But the majority of stuff we 'need' we can wait a little longer for. I find it really helpful to keep a wish list on my phone of things I would like. Recently that included frames for a gallery wall (I wrote down the sizes of the prints), a serving dish for veggies, some wellies and a mirror. I keep this list running so that when I am in a charity or second-hand shop, I don't get overwhelmed and can look only for the items I need. It has helped a lot and recently we've managed to source a whole load of frames and a mirror for the downstairs bathroom – all from the charity shop. So when you think,

'Ah, it would be good to have a winter coat!' write it down and see what you find next time you're out and about.

Get to know the charity shops

Knowing your local second-hand shops – which ones have more homeware, which ones often have a lot of clothes, and so on – can be very helpful when you're looking for a certain thing. There is one charity shop in Chipping Norton that I know will always have good china and glassware, and another that nearly always has some good photo frames. Different shops prioritise different products, so it can be helpful to get to know them.

It is also a great idea to get to know the staff. They will be able to tell you when new stock is coming in, what day they put things out or if something great is in the back. Make friends, stop for a chat and ask for help.

Buy online

Thrifting is so easy now thanks to the likes of Vinted, Depop, eBay and Facebook Marketplace. I try not to buy new these days, but I do still get new items from Vinted. For example, I am currently in need of a new pair of wellies. There's a particular brand I love, so I have been searching for new, with tags still on, in my size and I've found multiple pairs. Facebook Marketplace is one of my absolute favourites for homeware, and most of our lounge furniture items have been second-hand bargains from FB Marketplace. Try setting yourself up with accounts online and get searching for exactly what you need.

Try something new

Charity shops aren't the only places to buy second hand; opportunities are everywhere these days. Get searching for local clothes swaps, second-hand designer boutiques, vintage shops and markets, flea markets, car boot sales and auctions. You can find a lot of these online too if you prefer shopping from the sofa. I love Etsy for a bit of vintage shopping, and my in-laws have a lot of fun going to their local auction, which releases an online catalogue each month so you can have a good look at everything from the comfort of your own home.

Upcycle

Don't be afraid to buy second-hand clothes that don't quite fit. If you've fallen in love with a Harris tweed jacket but it's too big, you can easily have it taken in by a tailor or learn to do it yourself. Likewise, don't be afraid of a homeware project. There are so many ideas on Pinterest and YouTube for upcycling. If the item is from a charity shop, it's likely to be fairly cheap anyway, so if the project doesn't go to plan you haven't lost much and most things can be salvaged!

Buying new

Sometimes we need to buy new and there's nothing wrong with that. Not everyone is able to buy second hand, or feels comfortable doing so. I get it. But there is so much we can do when buying new, so here are a few tips.

Buy quality

When you're buying something new you want it to last as long as possible. Think of it as an investment piece that you can bring out year after year and even pass on to someone else when you're done with it. Choose high-quality products that you can repair when needed. Wax jackets are a great option for a coat, as they can be rewaxed. Wool coats can be de-pilled and repaired. A good quality pair of shoes can be re-soled. Try to save your money and buy good investment pieces that could last you a lifetime.

Look for sustainability

A decade ago, when I first started my sustainable-fashion journey, finding clothes from sustainable brands with transparent supply chains was very difficult. We still have a long way to go, but I am pleased to say that it is becoming more and more possible. There are now lots of brands that prioritise sustainable and ethical practices and these are a great option for buying new clothes.

Buy local

Here in the UK we have many wonderful small businesses. It's a great part of our culture and I would champion shopping 'small' every time.

Have a look at what's around you locally and in the UK as a whole. There are many small businesses making incredible items, from beautiful leather-work bags and belts to handmade shoes to stunning tweed jackets. When you're needing that new piece for your wardrobe, try looking closer to home first.

Make your own

I've been making my own clothes for years now and it has been a big part of my healing process (see Chapter 2). I have so enjoyed learning new skills and slowly forming my own handmade wardrobe with clothes I absolutely love and can wear over and over again.

Getting started

Here are some tips on how to get started on making your own clothes:

Pick a craft

It can be very tempting to try everything at once. Perhaps you want a cute crocheted top and a knitted hat, and also a pretty, handmade dress for Christmas. That's great, but if you try to take up too many new skills at once you'll get overwhelmed. Start by picking the craft you most want to learn – one that is accessible to you. For me, this was knitting. I spent a good deal of time getting to grips with knitting before moving on to my next craft skill, dressmaking. Don't give yourself too much to do all at once.

Ask for help

Making your own clothes has definitely skipped a generation. What was commonplace in our grandparents' era (well, mine at least – hello, those over thirty reading this book!) is now an unusual and often inaccessible hobby. Our parents' generation didn't pass the dressmaking and fibre-craft skills down; neither did most of us learn them at school. This may be leaving you at a loss as to where to start with your making journey, but I encourage you to ask around. I had no idea my auntie could knit before she taught me at ten years old. My sister Sarah taught me to thread a sewing machine, and countless other women have helped me along my making journey. Ask around among family and friends, and at church, to see who crafts. I bet it'll be a lot more people than you realise, and if there's one thing I can be sure of when it comes to a crafter, they are always willing to give you a hand to get started.

Look for advice online

Over the years I have learned so much from the online world. I have been inspired by social media to make and try things, and whenever I am stuck I simply pull up a YouTube or Skillshare video. It's like having a crafting instructor right there in your living room for whenever you need them.

Making sustainably

Okay, so now we are making our own clothes, but how do we ensure we are doing this sustainably for both us and the planet? Here are my top tips for sustainable making.

Buy second-hand supplies

This is good advice both for your wallet and for the planet, especially if you're a beginner. Craft supplies can be very costly and if you don't know what you're doing yet, you could end up wasting materials. Buying second-hand fabric in the form of bedsheets, tablecloths and curtains is a great way to save money and be more sustainable. You could also raid your cupboards for old bedsheets and ask around your friends and family.

Yarn is a little harder to find second hand, but most charity shops have a stash of donated yarn and sometimes you can come up trumps, so it is always worth asking. It's also worth asking people you know, as many of us start hobbies that we later give up, so there's normally a ball or two rolling around somewhere.

This also works well for sewing machines and other equipment. Knitting needles and crochet hooks are nearly always to be found in charity shops or at the back of a friend or relative's cupboard. Sewing machines can be bought online or in stores second hand, or borrowed from a friend. It's a great way to save money and check if you like doing something before investing too much.

Fibre content

When you make your own clothes, you get the opportunity to know exactly what is going into them. It becomes much easier to trace the supply chain when you are picking the materials you use. One way to ensure that the items you make are sustainable is by choosing natural fibres. Of course, this doesn't always work if you're buying second-hand supplies, but if you're buying new, try to use fibres that will biodegrade. Stay away from those acrylic fabrics, choosing instead 100% cotton, wool, linen and viscose. (By the way, did you know that linen is a great fabric for both summer and winter? Its unique air-trapping quality means it keeps you cool in the summer and warm in the winter! It will also biodegrade quickly, being a natural fibre.)

Similarly, when choosing yarn for making clothes, try to source natural fibres such as wool, alpaca, cotton, bamboo and linen. There are lots of beautiful indie yarn shops, many with great websites, so you'll find all sorts of yarns to choose from. Wool and alpaca are your best bets for warm winter clothing, whereas cotton, bamboo and linen yarns can make lovely knitted or crocheted garments for the summertime.

Deadstock

A deadstock fabric is one that has been commissioned and designed by a brand, used to make a collection of clothes and once the season for that collection is over, any left over is discarded. For a long time, this would end up in the bin (most likely in other countries, if you live in the UK), filling up landfill and causing harmful gases to be released. Luckily, we now have many deadstock fabric shops giving these fabrics a new lease of life.

Caring for your clothes

Whether you're making them or buying them, caring for your clothes is an important part of slowing your wardrobe down. Here are a few ways to look after your clothes the best you can and make them last for years and years.

Wash infrequently

The frequency with which we wash our clothes varies from person to person, but we have created a culture here in the UK of washing them far too often. Sometimes, such as after exercising, it is necessary to wash clothes after one wear, but for the most part we can get away with washing them a lot less. Washing our clothes frequently will shorten their lifespan hugely, so it is better to try to make them go as long as possible without washing. After wearing, leave your clothes out to air over night, then the next day do the sniff test. If they smell, give them a wash, obviously, but often they will have aired enough to wear again later in the week.

Wash correctly

Reading the label on clothes, or checking the band on a ball of yarn or label on a piece of fabric, is an important part of taking care of them. You want to make sure you are washing them correctly. We tend to wash our clothes on very hot cycles here in the UK and often this is completely unnecessary. Try washing at a lower temperature and see how you get on. You might have to experiment a few times, but you'll soon learn what your clothes need.

Learn to mend

Sewing on a button, fitting a new zip, patching up a hole – these are all useful skills to learn and will keep your clothes lasting for years and years. I recently attended a 'visible mending' workshop, and it was great to learn how to darn socks and fix a hole in my jeans with fun, decorative stitching. Check out YouTube, Skillshare and your local craft shops for tutorials on mending clothes.

Take care of your knitwear

Good quality knitwear, whether it's handmade, second hand or new from a sustainable source, needs to be taken care of. It is important to note that sheep's wool and alpaca fleece are antimicrobial, meaning the oils within the wool have bacteria-killing properties. This means that you really don't need to wash your woollen garments often. In fact it is worse for them, as you are washing out all of the natural oils and properties of the wool. Nearly all of my hand-knitted 100% wool garments are made to go over something such as a dress or T-shirt. This means they are never in direct contact with the skin, so I can get away with simply airing them out in between wears and washing them just once a year.

In about August/September time I will take out all the hand-knits in the house (we have them for me, my husband and the dog!) and I will start the process of handwashing them.

How to wash knitwear

Step 1: If you have a deep sink make sure it is clean, or if not use a plastic washing-up bowl (I have a special one just for knitwear). Fill it with luke-warm water. Add in some gentle handwashing laundry soap that is suitable for wool.

Step 2: Add your garment and completely submerge, gently moving it around in the water. Then leave to soak for twenty minutes.

Step 3: Drain the water, then carefully squeeze as much water as you can from the garment. Never wring out a knitted garment.

Step 4: Once you've squeezed as much water from it as you can (it will still be quite wet, but not pouring), take it over to a large dry towel lying flat on the floor. Lay your garment down flat and roll it up in the towel. Stand/kneel on the towel to absorb more water. Repeat this step as many times as you need to.

Step 5: Lie the garment out flat on a table or other surface near a heat source to dry. If you have an electric heated airer, this is perfect for drying knitwear, or if it is a nice day, you could lie it on a towel outside in the sun. Ideally, clean all your knitwear earlier in the year, before it gets too cold in the house and takes a long time to dry, which can cause clothes to smell musty.

However you decide to slow down your wardrobe, just remember that your clothes should feel like you. They should make you comfortable and happy, and give you confidence. The clothes you buy and make can help to change our planet, but go slowly; don't worry about doing it perfectly. We need lots of imperfect people buying sustainably rather than a few perfect people living sustainably.

SUMMER

A warm breeze,
bare feet on soft grass,
an ever-humming buzz of bees,
the first taste of a homegrown strawberry,
long lazy Sundays outside,
picnics and alfresco dinners,
warm walks at dusk and early slow mornings,
freckles on skin and dirt under fingernails,
deep breaths of fresh air and time to just be.

5
Nature

Some old-fashioned things like fresh air and sunshine are hard to beat.
(Laura Ingalls Wilder)[8]

But ask the animals, and they will teach you,
  or the birds in the sky, and they will tell you;
or speak to the earth, and it will teach you,
  or let the fish in the sea inform you.
Which of all these does not know
  that the hand of the Lord has done this?
In his hand is the life of every creature
  and the breath of all mankind.
(Job 12:7–10)

There was a time when the whole of life revolved around nature and the seasons. When all of us could identify a particular tree or bird or plant. We had to – it was essential for survival and to understand what was going on in the world around us. I absolutely love watching old TV series like *Little House on the Prairie*, where the characters frequently stand in fields and talk about the storm coming in and how they must prepare for it. They have learned to tell what the sudden change in wind means, or the morning frost, or the first leaf to fall. It is integral to their survival. These days, we've lost our connection to nature. Our fast-paced life, which never stops and continues for 365 days of the year, distracts us from what is going on around us. Children are much more likely to be able to name TV characters than identify tree species.

Back in 2017, nature writer and author Robert Macfarlane and illustrator Jackie Morris released a beautiful book called *The Lost Words*. These two creators had discovered that children in the UK were losing words – the words of the natural world. They set out to create a book that would teach and inspire children to once again find wonder in the natural world and learn all about the nature around them. I highly recommend this beautiful book, but it is not just children who need to reconnect with nature. In this chapter I want to encourage you too to go out and find the things we've lost. Explore nature with childish abandon and give your soul a little time to slow down and connect with your Creator.

The green stuff is good for us

When I was studying at university I started to suffer with anxiety. I would have panic attacks regularly and I soon found it quite hard to go about my days as normal. There wasn't a huge amount of understanding from those around me and I remember feeling very lost. I found myself craving nature and the countryside, discovering that the only place I really felt safe was outside, surrounded by green and away from all the noise.

It was during these years that I realised city life wasn't for me and that I was meant to become a country bumpkin from an early age. But this definitely isn't the case for everyone, and I know there are so many great benefits to living in a city or town. We are all uniquely made, which means our needs and desires around where we live are unique and different. I do, however, believe that we are all made to connect with nature and whether you are a country bumpkin like me or a city-dweller like many of my friends, we can all benefit hugely from 'the green stuff'.

There is so much info out there about why nature is good for us, I couldn't possibly fit it into one chapter. Instead, I've suggested a few other books about the benefits of getting out into green spaces (see Resources), so do have a read if you get chance. Scientific research has identified the following benefits of getting out into nature:

- It helps to strengthen the immune system.
- It reduces blood pressure and heart rate.
- It calms the nervous system.
- It can boost cognitive function and creativity.
- It can improve sleep and regulate our circadian rhythm.
- It can help with focus and bring clarity.
- Some studies have found it increases the natural killer cell activity that helps to fight tumours and cancer.
- It connects us with God and his planet, giving us a passion for protecting the earth.

Getting outside

Back in Chapter 1 we talked about our circadian rhythm and how important it is to help regulate this for a healthy nervous system. We also talked about getting natural light early in the day to help set this. Opening a window or stepping out onto a balcony or into a garden can be a great way to start our morning light journey. For a long time, this was the only way I could access the outside world, but we will feel so many benefits from getting outside, even if we just sit there for two minutes and take some deep breaths.

Later, when my health began to improve, I started going on a short walk with our rescue greyhound. Greyhounds are great dogs for the chronically ill and disabled, as they need very little exercise and are basically couch potatoes. They don't judge you at all for needing to rest a lot and, in fact, encourage napping pretty much all day long. When we first adopted Pearl, my husband would walk her twice a day. I was unable to manage any walking at all with her. But as I worked towards recovery and managing my chronic illness, I decided to try to get out with her for ten minutes each day. We started by walking around the cul-de-sac. It was the slowest walk you've ever seen an unaided twenty-five-year-old do, but after two years of barely being able to leave the house by myself it was a huge milestone for me.

I remember the first time we did it. It was a cold wet February day. The rain stopped briefly, so I popped on my coat and Pearl's, and we began shuffling along the pavement. She was, as ever, very patient with me and enjoyed some good sniffs as we went. It wasn't the most exciting walk, but I was proud of myself for doing it. Soon, we were managing a daily ten-minute walk, and those small steps in the fresh air became a bit of a lifeline. I started to notice the changing nature around me: little buds forming on the trees and the sound of birdsong getting louder.

Covid hit a month later and, within a few weeks, my husband was home all the time. He began to join me on our walks, and we started to go a little further each day. Soon I was making it out of the cul-de-sac and was able to marvel at the banks of daffodils in our village. There was a small piece of woodland – hardly worth calling woodland at all, just a scrap of trees – and it became my goal each day. It was 0.9 miles from the front door, round the 'woods' and back again. That spring, with the help of Pearl and my husband, I started regular walks there and back. It was such a treat after so long struggling alone indoors. I would notice all the flowers and blossom through the village on our way to the woods and then we would be encapsulated in the green leaves of hundreds of beech trees. Squirrels would dart left and right, sending Pearl into an excited frenzy, and I could feel myself calming down. Our village was right next to the A40, so it wasn't a particularly peaceful walk, but it was mine and I was managing it. I could feel my nervous system calm as I stepped out of the house and breathed in fresh air. Noticing the changing nature around me kept me centred in the present moment and my anxious mind stopped racing for the thirty minutes it would take me to walk.

We moved a year later to a much quieter village in the Cotswolds. There was no loud A40 road and it was here that I began to learn about the importance of morning light and our circadian rhythm. Until that point, I had walked Pearl in the afternoon. It was the last thing I did each day before crashing out. I think it was the right thing to do at that time, when I was first learning to exercise again, but once it had become an easier activity for me to do and was a regular part of my day, I decided to make it earlier, to incorporate it into my morning light routine. It was hard at first. Anyone who has struggled with a fatigue-related condition will tell you that getting out of bed in the morning can be very difficult. But soon Pearl and I were managing it.

Our walks start our day now. Me and Pearl. I can't imagine starting my day without one. They centre me, remind me of what is important, fill my lungs with fresh air, get my body moving, boost my immune system, calm my nervous system and keep me in the present moment. I don't listen to music or podcasts; I just walk. Sometimes I talk to Pearl. But most importantly, these walks remind me of who is in control. An almighty and incredible Creator. Each day I get to marvel at the beauty all around me that he created. These walks remind me to simply put one foot in front of the other, focusing on the one who created all the wonders of the earth but who still knows me by name.

Start your own nature rituals

It doesn't matter where you are based, whether it's a city or a croft on a far-flung Scottish island, everyone can benefit from getting out in nature and everyone can access it. It may mean travelling a bit, but it will be worth it in the end. Here are some ideas on how to start connecting with nature and building your own daily, weekly and monthly rituals.

A daily walk

My daily walk is probably the most important element of my day after my quiet time. I try my best to get out for at least twenty minutes every day, regardless of my symptoms. It can be hard when the rain is pelting down or it's really chilly in the winter, but getting out no matter what the weather is a very good way to break up your day and take care of yourself. This is where having a dog that wants a walk can be very helpful! But if you are without a dog, you will just have to motivate yourself for walkies. Find a time that works best for you. That might be first thing, or perhaps at lunchtime to take some time away from your desk, or maybe in the evening after dinner to help you digest your food. Whatever time is best for your schedule try to stick to it. Keep it in there as a non-negotiable, even if it is just ten minutes. It takes about three weeks before something becomes a habit, so if you go out and walk around the block, noticing the trees or the birds for only ten minutes a day, it should become a habit quite quickly, and your body will begin to crave that outside time.

Forest bathing

Forest bathing, or shinrin-yoku, is a Japanese mindfulness exercise practised for generations. The idea is very simple: you go into the forest or a park with trees, or even just find a nice tree in your garden, and spend some time soaking up the atmosphere, breathing, meditating and centring yourself in the present moment.

This outdoor activity is quite an accessible one, as most of us can find a tree somewhere. Here are my suggestions for how to get started with forest bathing:

- Find some woodland or a park, or if you can't find either, simply find a tree you can sit under without being disturbed.
- Turn your phone off and put it in your pocket or bag. Don't get it out for at least five minutes!
- Close your eyes and take three deep, calming breaths: in for four, hold for two, out for six.
- Open your eyes and look up at the canopy of trees above you. If you can lie down that would be even better.
- See what you notice. Maybe it's how the light falls through the leaves, or the colours changing, or perhaps the different thicknesses of branches. Maybe you can see buds forming or leaves beginning to turn orange. Spend some time telling yourself about all the things you notice.
- Think about how you feel after this. Are you calmer? Are you more present? It's good to notice the effects this has so that you know what to do for your body in future.

Grounding

Having been housebound myself for a while and still often struggling to find enough energy to leave my home, I know how important accessing nature can be. If you're finding it hard to get out but you have a garden space, no matter how small, grounding can be a great way to get a bit of a nature fix. All you have to do is take your shoes and socks off and place your bare feet on the earth. That's it. You don't even need to stand if standing isn't something you are able to do. You just need to directly connect your feet with God's earth.

Take deep breaths, bring yourself into the present moment and push your weight down into your feet. Take time to notice how the ground feels beneath you. Can you hear anything? Perhaps the sun is warming your face, or there is a chill in the air. Noticing all this can help bring you into the present moment.

Grounding is a great daily practice, especially if walking or getting out into nature isn't as easy for you. You can still benefit hugely from this time outside.

Spending time around water

Along with all the research on the positive effects of green spaces on our mental and physical health, studies have also shown that blue spaces can have just as much of a positive impact. Looking at water, be it the sea, a river, an estuary, a lake or even a simple pond, is clinically proven to improve well-being. And looking at moving water in the form of a river, the sea or a waterfall can help to lower blood pressure and calm the nervous system. Here are some ideas on how you can enjoy the blue spaces around you.

Wild swimming

Swimming outdoors has once again become a popular pastime, with thousands of us taking to the great outdoor swimming spots we have available all over the UK. I am a huge fan of a wild swim and regularly use our local river, or the tidal pools when visiting my family in Fife, Scotland. There are lots of ways to begin wild swimming, but here's some info to get you started safely.

- *Find a designated spot.* It isn't always safe to just jump in anywhere, so I would always suggest choosing a well-known wild-swimming area to begin with. There are many websites sharing the best places to go, with advice on how to enter the water (check out the Resources page for a good book on wild-swimming spots in England and Wales).
- *Take someone with you.* It's not advisable to go alone. There are lots of wild-swimming groups all over the UK, so why not try joining one of these?

- *Grab the gear.* It's important to make sure you've got all you need, as wild swimming can be quite a cold affair. Make sure you warm up afterwards with a hot drink, plenty of cosy clothing and something to eat.

Other options for enjoying the water

- Kayaking
- Rowing
- Paddling
- Mud larking
- Shell collecting
- A simple stroll along the river

Nature in winter

Accessing nature in the wintertime can be hard for a lot of people. The cold and the wet keep us indoors and the late mornings and dark evenings mean we get even less light and hardly any vitamin D. But it is so important to continue getting outside throughout the winter season. My chronic pain is often made worse by cold weather, but winter walks have been some of my favourites. I love taking Pearl for a stroll on a frosty morning, when the world isn't yet properly awake and both of us are trussed up in our hand-knitted jumpers. I marvel at how delicately the frost touches the plants and trees, even coating the cobwebs in an icy dusting that glints in the cold sunshine.

There's no such thing as bad weather, only bad clothing

This is such a British saying … and completely untrue. There *is* such a thing as bad weather. I am very much not a 'struggle through the wind and rain' kind of girl. I am a 'snuggle up and have a hot chocolate while watching the rain and think about going for a walk tomorrow instead' girl. I do, however, concede that having the right clothing can make a world of difference, especially in the winter.

If you struggle to get out at this time of year, I suggest investing in a few pieces that will make it easier. A good duvet coat, as I like to call it (a full-length puffer coat), has allowed me to walk Pearl no matter what the temperature and stay lovely and cosy while doing so. I may look like a walking sleeping bag, but this helps my chronic pain immensely and I can still get my morning-light fix even at –7°C (true story!).

I would also recommend investing in wellies if you live in a muddy part of the country, a good waterproof coat and trousers, walking boots, snow boots for those freezing icy days when you worry that walking the dog might mean you losing a toe, and of course knit yourself plenty of hats, mittens, scarfs and gloves!

I know that winter clothing can be expensive, but there are lots of second-hand options and there really is nothing more important than investing in your mental and physical health. Getting outdoors in the winter can make the world of difference to your health and I think we should all be trying to do a little bit more of it.

Stargazing

A lot of activities stop in the winter for many of us. I am not a winter wild swimmer, as the cold is too much for my chronic pain to cope with, and I don't get my kayak out once we hit November (although if you love a winter paddle, go for it!). I still go for lots of walks, and I would always recommend this, but the early, dark evenings do limit you somewhat. The winter does, however, open easier opportunities for stargazing, and with the sun setting by 4:30 p.m. in the UK in November, this is one the whole family can get involved in. Wrap up warm and make it a fun evening out with a flask of hot chocolate, some binoculars and plenty of blankets to lie on top of.

Winter solstice

The winter solstice is an ancient pagan festival that was celebrated for many years in the UK. It marks the shortest day of the year, welcoming in the darkness and looking forward towards the days lengthening and welcoming in the light. It was a big part of our year when our lives were dictated by the seasons. It takes place on 21 December, just before Christmas, and indeed our celebrations of Christmas were set at this time of year due to the original festival of light in this country.

A lot of Christians are unsure about pagan festivals, but I think it can be positive for us all to approach them as an opportunity to take stock of the season and thank God for the moment. It is important that we connect with the seasons, with God's creation, and take the opportunity to slow down. Celebrating the winter solstice can also be very helpful for those struggling with the dark evenings and is an encouragement to look towards the Light of the world.

Here are some ideas for celebrating the winter solstice:

- Take a walk to watch the sun set. This is fairly easy to do in the UK, as it will happen between 3 and 4 p.m., depending on where you are. Find a good hill or high point to get the best view. This is a lovely activity to do with friends or family. You can make it quite the occasion by taking along a flask of something hot, maybe even a Christmassy nibble or two! Remember to take torches for getting home, as it'll be dark.
- Light a fire or candles and celebrate the light returning, to remind you of the Light of our world, Jesus. This is a great time to load up the fire pit and huddle around a bonfire.
- Host a candlelit dinner around the fire pit. There's nothing better than snuggling up around a fire in the winter, all huddled in winter coats with blankets wrapped around you. Enjoy hot soup and toasted marshmallows as you gaze up at the night sky and know that the days are lengthening, and light will be returning to the land once more.

Throughout the seasons

Here are some things to see and do throughout the seasons:

Spring

- Birds building nests
- Daffodil walks (check out daffodil walks all over the UK)
- Ducklings at the local pond
- Blossom trees
- Bluebell woods

- Wild garlic (see Chapter 7)
- Tulip gardens
- May blossom in the hedgerows

Summer

- Cow parsley
- Elderflowers
- Signal crayfishing
- Wild swimming
- Beach days
- Wildflower meadows
- Picnics and cooking outside

Autumn

- Leaves changing
- Conkers
- Blackberries, elderberries, sloes and damsons
- Plenty of foraging (see Chapter 7)
- Leaf collecting/kicking
- Muddy walks and puddle splashing
- Pheasants everywhere

Winter

- Solstice sunset
- Frosty walks
- First snow
- Sunrise
- First snowdrops (check out snowdrop walks all over the UK)

Accessing nature is important for everyone and I hope this chapter has helped to inspire you to find ways to get outside and connect with God and his creation.

6
Entertainment and community

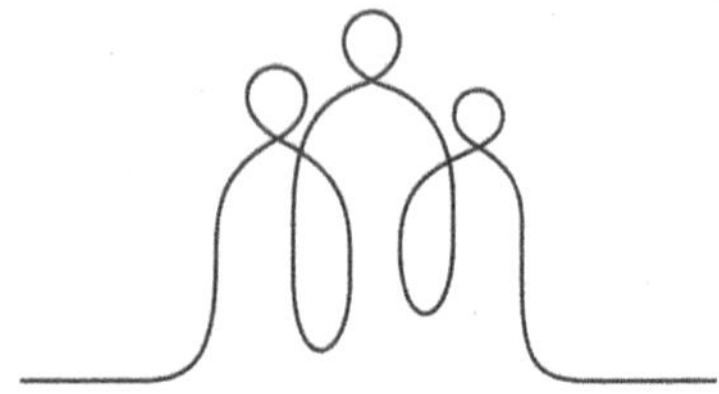

> The power of finding beauty in the humblest things makes home happy and life lovely.
> (Louisa May Alcott)[9]

> Finally, brothers and sisters, whatever is true, whatever is noble, whatever is right, whatever is pure, whatever is lovely, whatever is admirable – if anything is excellent or praiseworthy – think about such things.
> (Philippians 4:8)

There is a famous quote attributed to Albert Einstein: 'Insanity is doing the same thing over and over and expecting different results.' I must say, I'm not sure this is a blanket rule. When it comes to training a puppy, yes, it can feel as though you are going insane as you repeatedly go through training again and again and again, sometimes waiting months for it to finally take hold in the doggo's mind (any puppy owners out there, I feel for you, but you'll get there in the end, don't worry!). I do think it applies to our lifestyle, though. If we are constantly exhausted, burnt-out and struggling but continue to live our lives in the same way again and again, how can we expect to feel any different?

How many of us are guilty of saying, 'I just need to get over this slump,' or, 'I just need to get this work project out of the way'? Or maybe it's, 'I just need to get to this holiday/that celebration/this month of the year'? On and on it goes. As a society we seem to be living in a perpetual state of 'it'll get better after …'. But it never actually does slow down or get better. Perhaps we need to re-evaluate and change things up in order for them to improve.

A great way to do this is to take a look at what we spend our time on. I'm not talking about our jobs or our family responsibilities – although these would definitely benefit from regular rigorous examination as to whether or not they are serving us and our families in the best way. I think a good place to start when it comes to slowing down our lives is what we are filling them with in our 'spare' time.

I've spent a lot of time watching TV. Much more than I wanted to. It is common among those who struggle with a chronic fatigue condition. We need regular rest time and effective distraction from chronic pain. When I first became unwell, I was watching TV pretty much all day in a bid to distract myself from the disabling pain. Over the years, though, I have managed to cut this down bit by bit and find other ways to rest and recharge.

Having said that, resting in front of a good TV show can be an integral part of living with disabling illness, so instead of trying to cut it out completely I have, over the years, become a lot more intentional about what I am consuming. I found that watching TV or listening to audiobooks that inspired me and reminded me of the life I was hoping to live when I began to heal from illness (it is very important as someone with ME/CFS to believe you will one day heal) was much more effective in my healing process than if I just watched trashy programmes that distracted me from the difficulties of life. It was around 2020 that I began watching more TV programmes on gardening, renovations of country homes, crafting podcasts on YouTube and even programmes on farming (I cannot get enough of these!). These TV shows reminded me of the life I'd been aspiring to for years. A life of slow country living, where you made do and mended, had a go at making things, and focused on family and community. I was inspired, learned new skills and found out an awful lot about sheep!

There is sometimes the need for a bit of trash TV, but what we spend our time watching, reading and listening to can really affect our nervous system and how we live out our lives. So many books, films, TV programmes and pieces of music glorify the fast-paced life. They show us flashy materialistic ways to live, and highlight all the things we don't have. As Christians it is important that we fill our lives with 'whatever is true, whatever is noble, whatever is right, whatever is pure, whatever is lovely, whatever is admirable ... excellent or praiseworthy' (Philippians 4:8). Every time we turn the TV on, open a book or pick a music station, we are making a choice. We have the power to slow our lives right down and it can start with what we're filling our time with.

Entertainment

I'm going to share a few of my favourite forms of entertainment for slow, quiet living – things that have encouraged and inspired me along my journey. Of course, we are all different and will have very different interests, but I hope some of these will fill your homes, thoughts and hearts with a slower and simpler way of life.

Some favourites over the years

Books

- *Little Women* by Louisa May Alcott
- All six Jane Austen novels
- *Anne of Green Gables* by L. M. Montgomery
- *The Ruthless Elimination of Hurry* by John Mark Comer
- *The Yorkshire Shepherdess* series by Amanda Owen
- *A Honeybee Heart Has Five Openings* by Helen Jukes
- The Chronicles of Narnia by C. S. Lewis
- *Holy Hygge* by Jamie Erickson
- *The Secret Garden* by F. H. Burnett
- *The Railway Children* by E. Nesbit

TV shows

- *The Good Life* (1975–8)
- *The Darling Buds of May* (1991)
- *Our Yorkshire Farm* (2018)

- *Little Women* (2017)
- *Our Farm Next Door* (2024)
- *All Creatures Great and Small* (2020)
- *Agatha Christie's Poirot* (1989)
- *Pride and Prejudice* (1995)
- *Miss Marple* (1984, 2004)
- *Little House on the Prairie* (1974)

Films

- *Little Women* (1994, 2019)
- *Pride and Prejudice* (2005)
- *The Guernsey Literary and Potato Peel Society* (2018)
- *Sense and Sensibility* (1995)
- *Under the Tuscan Sun* (2003)
- *A Room with a View* (1985)
- *Enchanted April* (1991)

Other slow and restful ways to spend your time

- Making puzzles
- Doing crafts
- Baking
- Gardening
- Playing board games
- Listening to the radio (my favourite station will always be Classic FM!)

Social media and screen time

We've already talked about our unhealthy addiction to our phones and how to get a bit more control over usage back in the section on Lent, but we couldn't have a chapter on entertainment without mentioning them again. It is estimated that in the UK we spend on average just under four hours on our phones each day. That is a huge amount of time. And if you don't believe me, this is really easy to check. Most phones will tell you your average daily usage and I must admit I find the number rather scary.

It can be very difficult to reduce this, because for many of us (myself included) our phones are used for work, for connecting with family and friends and to get us from A to B. They are such useful devices. I also use mine every day to listen to life-giving audiobooks, meditations and daily devotionals. But we do seem to have a tendency to be at the mercy of our phones.

A few years ago, I started to notice that whenever I picked up my phone, my husband would pick up his too and vice versa. I bet you're doing the same. As soon as you see someone with their phone, you're reaching for yours. And it's not just seeing others on their phones. I seem to have a compulsion to pick it up nearly every fifteen minutes. As a child I would sit and craft or read for hours and hours uninterrupted. Now I can't go thirty minutes without checking notifications.

Studies show that the constant barrage of information coming from our phones in the form of social media and other communication can heighten our nervous system. It is putting us on high alert, waiting for the next thing and then the next thing. There have also been lots of studies to show that the likes and comments we get on social media offer little dopamine kicks, leaving us always wanting more and more.

It is no secret that social media is designed to attract us and then keep us there for as long as possible. It is playing havoc with our attention span, causing us a deep sense of inadequacy and overloading our system with far more information than we were ever meant to know or understand.

I love Instagram and YouTube – they are part of my work and I find them very inspiring – but I think it is vitally important that we take control and do not let things run wild. It is up to us to set boundaries and parameters on both *how much* we are viewing and *what* we are viewing. I encourage you to ask yourself what exactly you're trying to get out of social media. Are you logging on and finding yourself inspired, or are you overwhelmed? Are you encouraged, or are you comparing your life to those of others? A great way to get a handle on this is to unfollow or mute unhelpful accounts. They may seem like the most harmless accounts in the world, but if you're finding yourself constantly making comparisons, this is not good.

I will regularly unfollow accounts that no longer serve me or are not promoting the kind of lifestyle I want to see. I try to regularly keep on top of what I am consuming online. Spend some time curating your feed, making sure you are following people you really want to follow, who are life-giving and helpful to you.

Cutting back

In Chapter 1 we looked at turning off our phones at the same time each night and leaving them out of the bedroom. I strongly recommend doing this, but if you'd like to take it one step further, you could incorporate a phone-free or social-media-free time into your schedule. It is entirely up to you how often you want to do this, or for how long, but I know there has been a lot of success with the Offline48 movement. The idea is that you turn your phone or social media off on Friday night and don't turn it back on until Sunday evening. That way you unplug from the virtual world for a whole weekend. Some people do this every weekend, others once a month and others whenever they feel they need to.

I have started to try to practise a social-media-free Sabbath, which is just twenty-four hours but works well for me. I am also a big fan of going off social media for holidays such as Christmas and Easter, when I want to spend uninterrupted time with my family. I find I have little to no self-control, so the best option for me is just to delete all the apps during this time.

Again, if you want to go further, you could also try going away on holiday and intentionally leaving your phone turned off. If you need a more guided version, there are lots of beautiful off-grid cabins, treehouses and camping spaces all over the UK, where they encourage you to switch off and leave your devices at the door, even locking them in a box in some cases. Everyone is different and has different needs, so make a choice as to what works best for you. But taking a good look at your consumption and trying to reduce it can make a huge difference to how you feel.

Something I personally have begun to learn recently is that despite what our society says, not everything has to be documented. We can survive without taking a photo or making a video of an event. It is healthy and normal for some things to exist only in our memory, and yes, we may forget them but that's okay. We won't forget the feeling of that good time or reap any fewer benefits. But continuing to live all our experiences through the lens of our phone will lessen the benefits and our enjoyment of life. I know I want to work towards being more present and just enjoying the moment rather than always trying to capture it to share with people later. It can be hard, but let's all try to work on it together.

Community

> And let us consider how we may spur one another on towards love and good deeds, not giving up meeting together, as some are in the habit of doing, but encouraging one another – and all the more as you see the Day approaching.
> (Hebrews 10:24–25)

A big part of slowing down and simplifying our lives is learning to lean on others more. We live in a very 'I'-centred society. When it comes to 'dealing' with life's problems, independence and self-sufficiency are seen as positives. Being honest, showing what is really going on and sharing how much we are struggling, is seen as a weakness. But this isn't how God made us to be. We are meant to live in community together.

Humans are born with a deep desire for love and connection. It comes from our intrinsic desire to know God and have a relationship with him. He built us in this way so we can come to know him. But he also built us in this way so we can come to know and love each other.

The world glorifies romantic love – we see it everywhere, in all the books, TV shows and films. And while romantic love is wonderful and a beautiful gift from God, it isn't enough on its own. We need a community of people to surround us for any marriage to thrive. We don't, however, need a marriage in order to thrive in a community of people. So perhaps community is something we need to strive for more.

Get to know the neighbours

Many of us have heard from our grandparents just how different life used to be. How neighbours stopped to talk with one another, and you knew the names of everyone on your street (depending on how long your street was). But these days you'd be lucky to even get to chat to the person in the house right next door. We are all so busy with our lives, desperate to get on with our day, that we never bother to stop and chat and get to know each other.

But what if we weren't? What if we slowed down enough to learn the name of the person next door? Or even have a chat to them? What if we got to know our colleagues better, or the man who always drives us to work on the bus? And this isn't to say anything of the church family we should be connecting with on a weekly basis.

Spending time with others and creating community is a very important part of living a slower life. It is key to our mental health, and it allows us to always have a 'village' not only in times of trouble but also in times of joy. Imagine how different all our lives would be if we were there to help each other out – if we watched our neighbour's dog for a few hours and then they popped the bins out for us while we were on holiday. Imagine how great the world would be if people could count on others to help out. I believe that this is something many of us want. Of course, there is the odd exception, but studies show that millennials are one of the loneliest generations ever to have lived. We have more possessions than at any other time in history, but we are more alone than ever.

We can change this. Perhaps it could start with you. I know it can feel like a daunting prospect, but why not ask your neighbour if you can borrow a wheelbarrow, a couple of eggs or a cup of sugar (the classic)? Being vulnerable can open up conversations, and it could lead to a real, lasting friendship. It is also a great way to build community and share some Christian generosity.

Gather

As humans, we love to gather together. I don't know of a single culture that doesn't have some kind of regular celebration or family get-together. In my family and my husband's, we use any excuse to celebrate, cook delicious food and bring people together. From games nights to dinner parties to pudding evenings with the girls, these gatherings are always a wonderful opportunity to slow down, connect and live in the present moment. Here are some ideas for gathering people throughout the seasons. Some of these will work across the seasons too!

Spring

- Mark the spring equinox with a tea party. Dress the house with daffodils, and celebrate the new season beginning and light returning

to the land. If you have access to some delicious wild garlic, why not try the recipe for wild garlic and cheese scones given below?
- Plan Easter gatherings (see 'Seasonal celebrations: Easter' for ideas).
- Arrange a group walk through the May blossom and enjoy the stunning sight of the countryside dressing itself in white.

Summer

- Have a beach BBQ – always a great idea at this time of year, but make sure you do it responsibly. Use safe equipment and check local rules for this.
- Organise a summertime pot-luck picnic – a fun and inclusive activity. Choose a spot that is easy for everyone to get to (this may even be your back garden – it doesn't really matter) and tell everyone to bring a seasonal dish to share. The incredible array of summer flavours on offer will be such a treat and you'll probably have leftovers for days!
- Play games in the park. Summer was made for this! Gather a group and bring along equipment for badminton, football, cricket, rounders – whatever you've got in the back of the cupboard. An assortment of games all afternoon is a great way to connect with people.
- Volunteer at a community garden project for the afternoon and meet some new people.

Autumn

- Host a celebration. As Christians we don't really celebrate Halloween, but I do love to celebrate autumn. It is such a beautiful time of year, so why not have an autumnal dinner party? You could follow the traditional style of Samhain, which celebrates the end of summer, accepting that all things must die away in the end to create new life in the spring. Host a Samhain supper with delicious autumnal dishes, and create a cute centrepiece with pumpkins and tealights.
- Go on a leafy walk with your friends or family to enjoy the beautiful changing colours.
- Host a bonfire and serve up marshmallows on sticks to toast on the fire. You could even go one step further and pop them between two chocolate digestives to make s'mores.

- Have a bulb-planting afternoon, where you and friends gather to plant bulbs into pots ready for the spring. You could choose pretty bowls (check out the charity shops if you don't have any) and plant up snowdrops ready to have as a centrepiece inside your home in the spring, or try planting up outdoor pots full of daffodils and tulips for a beautiful display in the garden or on a balcony.

Winter

- Host a candlelit solstice dinner party. It doesn't need to be fancy – order a takeaway if you want to! Turn all the lights off and enjoy the glow of the flames.
- Have an Epiphany tart-making session (see 'Seasonal Celebrations: Epiphany' for recipe).
- Host a Galentine's pudding evening with all your girlfriends (or Palentines if you're a guy). Everyone brings a pudding to share and a note saying what they love about someone there. These are placed in a pot and read out anonymously. Everyone goes away feeling full and loved. What could be better?
- Go on family walks to see snowdrops. There are plenty of snowdrop gardens all over the UK, but you'll probably know of other patches near you. It is lovely to get outside in those colder months and see a beautiful sign of hope.
- Watch the sunrise or sunset with others.

The seasons and celebrations throughout our year can help to encourage us to gather and spend time together – to carve out time in our busy schedules, slow down and rest in each other's company. But you don't need a reason to gather. Be the one to reach out and bring people together, even if it's just for a super-relaxed evening of pasta bake and a natter in front of *Strictly Come Dancing*. I promise you won't regret it.

Recipe for wild garlic and cheese scones

Serves 8–10

Ingredients

- 450 g self-raising flour
- 2 tsp baking powder
- 100 g cold butter, cut into cubes
- 200 g cheddar cheese, grated
- 300 ml milk, plus a little extra for brushing
- 60 g (ish) wild garlic leaves

Method

1. Thoroughly wash and finely chop the garlic leaves and leave to dry a little.
2. Preheat the oven to 220°C/200°C fan/gas 7 and line a couple of baking trays with baking paper.
3. Mix the flour and baking powder together. Add the butter and using your fingertips rub it into the flour until the mixture resembles breadcrumbs.
4. Add 150 g of the cheese and all the wild garlic. Mix until well combined.
5. Pour the milk into the mixture, and using the flat of a dinner knife bring it together until a dough forms. Roll the dough around the bowl to pick up any crumbs that aren't incorporated.
6. Dust a clean work surface with flour and gently press the ball out into a rough square about 2.5–3 cm thick.
7. Use a cookie cutter to cut out the scones, and pop them onto the prepared baking trays. Repeat until you have used up all the mixture.

8. Brush each scone with a little milk, then sprinkle some cheddar on top.
9. Bake in the oven for 12–15 minutes until they are well risen and golden brown on top.
10. Leave to cool on a rack and then enjoy with lots of butter!

AUTUMN

Crunchy leaves and russet trees,
hot chocolate and s'mores,
chestnuts, conkers and the last mushrooms,
smoky village bonfires and crackling fireworks,
root vegetable soups and warming stews left to cook all day,
open fires, crafting and cosying up under blankets,
hand-knit socks and muddy boots,
nature slowing down, nests built and the start of a long sleep.

Seasonal celebrations: Harvest

Growing up in the Church of England, harvest was a big celebration. I remember the beautiful displays created by the talented women on the flower rota; dried flowers and wheat sheaves displayed on the altar. We also had a wooden plaited loaf of bread on display, a nod to the days when there would have been a fresh plaited loaf baked and presented on the altar to celebrate this festival.

Harvest was a time of generosity, when we were encouraged to bring bags full of food to donate to the local mission our church supported. I imagine that when this festival first began in the Church of England back in the Victorian era, it was a much prettier sight, with baskets filled with fruit and vegetables going spare from a bumper harvest.

Of course, it is important to be generous all year round. It is a part of our walk with Jesus, and I am pleased to say that some of the most generous people I know are Christians. I am for ever humbled by the ease with which they give their money, time and energy. But harvest is a wonderful time to remember all we have, thank God for it and look at how we might reach out and help others who are struggling. It's a key point in the year to take stock and remember to give generously.

The story of Ruth

One of my favourite stories in the Bible is that of Ruth – a woman born outside of God's people and yet he used her to play a key role in history. Her story is one of true faith and devotion, and of God's incredible redeeming power. If you aren't familiar with the story, I highly recommend reading the book of Ruth in the Bible. But to summarise, Ruth was the daughter-in-law of Naomi, a Jewish woman. Naomi, along with her husband and two sons, left her community and moved to Moab. Both her sons married Moabite women, and one of these was Ruth. This went against the strict law that Jews shouldn't marry Gentiles.

Disaster struck, and Naomi's husband and two sons all died. She sent her daughters-in-law away back to their families, telling them she would return to the town where she was from and re-join her people as a widow. Ruth refused to leave her and instead devoted all her energy to taking care of Naomi. To help feed them, Ruth participated in a practice called gleaning, where the women picked up all the bits of wheat that were missed by the male harvesters and were allowed to keep them for free to help feed their families through the winter. This was common around the world for thousands of years and was a lifeline for many. In fact, in many countries this practice still takes place and is encouraged to help combat food waste.

Ruth began gleaning in Boaz's field, not realising that he was in fact her deceased husband's close relative. In this passage we see them meet for the first time:

> Boaz asked the overseer of his harvesters, 'Who does that young woman belong to?'
>
> The overseer replied, 'She is the Moabite who came back from Moab with Naomi. She said, "Please let me glean and gather among the sheaves behind the harvesters." She came into the field and has remained here from morning till now, except for a short rest in the shelter.'
>
> So Boaz said to Ruth, 'My daughter, listen to me. Don't go and glean in another field and don't go away from here. Stay here with the women who work for me. Watch the field where the men are harvesting and follow along after the women. I have told the men not to lay a hand on you. And whenever you are thirsty, go and get a drink from the water jars the men have filled.'
>
> At this, she bowed down with her face to the ground. She asked him, 'Why have I found such favour in your eyes that you notice me – a foreigner?'

Boaz replied, 'I've been told all about what you have done for your mother-in-law since the death of your husband – how you left your father and mother and your homeland and came to live with a people you did not know before. May the LORD repay you for what you have done. May you be richly rewarded by the LORD, the God of Israel, under whose wings you have come to take refuge.'

'May I continue to find favour in your eyes, my lord,' she said. 'You have put me at ease by speaking kindly to your servant – though I do not have the standing of one of your servants.'

At mealtime Boaz said to her, 'Come over here. Have some bread and dip it in the wine vinegar.'

When she sat down with the harvesters, he offered her some roasted grain. She ate all she wanted and had some left over. As she got up to glean, Boaz gave orders to his men, 'Let her gather among the sheaves and don't reprimand her. Even pull out some stalks for her from the bundles and leave them for her to pick up, and don't rebuke her.'

So Ruth gleaned in the field until evening.
(Ruth 2:5–17)

The story of Ruth has so many exciting twists and turns, and in the end Boaz and Ruth get married. Boaz's generosity and Ruth's obedience and devotion are the stalwarts of this story and teach us so much about living out God's love in real life.

My suggestion is that you read the story of Ruth and pray about how God might be calling you to be generous in this season.

Slow generosity

Generous living isn't just about money, although it is great to help financially where you can. For many Christians it is also about giving our time and energy. All of this is a part of the generous living that God calls us to. But it is important not to get so wrapped up in the giving of yourself that you end up running around in a whirl. In recent years, the trend of always being busy and rushing from place to place has crept into the Church, and sometimes I think we forget what is important and why we are doing the things we do.

When I became chronically ill and disabled, I was unable to give in the same way I had before. I lost my job, so this made it harder to give financially, but I was also unable to take part in the activities I had done before. I couldn't help with children's work at church or serve on the coffee rota or volunteer at a mission. I was limited in my ability to give and I found it hard to find space within the Church to still be of use as a chronically ill and disabled person.

But God creates space for us all. It may take some people more time to do a task, but this should not exclude them from doing it. Our world is moving too fast and although I would never wish for illness, I appreciate that it taught me the importance of slowing down, and helped me to find ways to give that don't require me to run around like a headless chicken.

Here are some slow and simple ways in which we can give:

- Cooking meals for people is a great way to give slowly. You can pick a time that works well for you, when you can cook slowly. If this is too far in advance, then you can freeze the meal and get it out for whoever needs it. And don't just wait for the big occasions: the birth of a baby, the death of a loved one, the big hospital operations. A meal can be so helpful at these times, but it can also be a real blessing to take food over to a friend who is just going through her normal week, and getting a home-cooked meal means an easy night after work.
- There is nothing better than a freshly baked loaf of bread! I bake bread every week and I love the smell, texture and taste. It makes a wonderful gift and can bless someone who is struggling. It is also a great opener for gifting to neighbours and having some chats over the garden fence!
- If you have decided to grow some food (see Chapter 3) you may end up with a lot more than you can eat! Every year we have more courgettes than I know what to do with and even after making fritters, cakes, chutneys and paellas they just keep coming! This is the perfect time to be generous. Perhaps set up a basket in front of your house with a sign telling people to help themselves. We regularly see this around our neighbourhood during the glut seasons for apples, pears and courgettes. Another option is to pack up a basket with

your delicious homegrown produce and take it over to a friend, neighbour or just someone you know who would appreciate it. In the past I have been gifted big stems of rhubarb tied with ribbon, and bowls full of homegrown strawberries, and it is always such a lovely treat. I think it is also important to remember that you don't have to wait for a glut in order to give. We are called to be generous with all we have, not just from our abundance and leftovers.

- Use your skills to bless someone. Be it crafting, sewing, baking or mechanics – whatever it is you're good at – offer to help someone who isn't as good at those things. We all have God-given talents and we are all different. That's what makes it so great when we come together. You could knit a jumper for a little one at church, or teach a friend or their child to use a sewing machine. My husband once went to fix our friend's car so they didn't have to take it to a garage. You could teach a young person who is newly living on their own how to cook a meal from scratch, or maybe you could mow the lawn of a busy person who just doesn't have the time to do it. The list of ways to help is endless, but look at the gifts God has given you (there will be many, I assure you) and think about how you could use them to bless someone.

Butternut squash lasagne

Serves 4–6 (and great for giving to someone else)

Ingredients

- 1 large squash or multiple smaller ones
- Dry lasagne sheets
- 500 ml passata
- 200 g spinach
- 2 large garlic cloves, crushed
- 1 red onion, chopped
- Olive oil
- 200 g extra-mature cheddar cheese, grated
- 200 ml milk
- 25 g butter (approx.)
- Plain flour

Method

1 Preheat the oven to 200°C/180°C fan/gas 6. Once up to temperature, begin by roasting the squash whole. How long you do this for will depend on the size of the squash. If you're using a large one, I would recommend 1.5–2 hours. You can check if the squash is ready by stabbing it with a knife. If the knife slips through easily, it's ready. You should be able to easily cut the squash in half and scoop out the insides. Discard any seeds.

2 Pop a large heavy-based skillet pan on the hob with a glug of olive oil in it. Once hot, add the red onion and cook on a medium heat until the onion begins to go translucent. Add the crushed garlic and cook for 1–2 minutes, being careful not to burn the garlic.

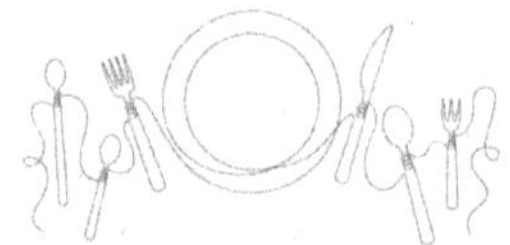

3 Add the flesh of the squash to the pan and stir through. If it's very thick you might want to add a little water to make this into more of a purée. Leave to cook for a few minutes.
4 Add some salt and pepper, then a good few handfuls of spinach. It's up to you how much you add. (I don't like too much, but my husband loves it.)
5 Turn the heat right down and pop the lid on, leaving the spinach to wilt.
6 Now start on the cheese sauce. Heat a knob of butter (about 25 g) in a saucepan on a low heat. Once melted, add a couple of tablespoons of plain flour and stir until it becomes a paste. If it is too thick, add a little more butter; if too thin, add a little more flour.
7 Once your paste is ready, slowly add the milk a little at a time, whisking it with your butter. This can be hard at first as it becomes quite thick, but keep going and eventually you will have a thick sauce. You might not need all the milk, so keep an eye on it and don't let it get too watery. You want it to be the consistency of yoghurt.
8 Add a little salt and pepper, then begin to add the cheese, a small handful at a time, whisking in between and allowing it to melt. I find this is best done by taste, so keep tasting the sauce until you feel it is cheesy enough. Again, you might not need all the cheese, or you might want a little bit more. I love a very cheesy sauce for my lasagne!
9 Once the cheese sauce is cheesy enough, remove it from the heat and set it aside. The spinach will be wilted by now and you should be able to stir it through your squash mixture. Take this off the heat also.
10 Now begin layering your lasagne. Take a rectangular dish and start by pouring a small layer of passata onto the

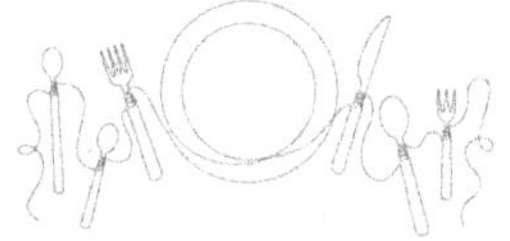

bottom of the dish. This shouldn't be too thick, but should cover the whole of the dish.

11 Then layer one third of the butternut mix on top, spreading it out evenly.

12 Cover this in one third of the cheese sauce and follow that up with the dried lasagne sheets. You might need to snap these to make them the right size to fit.

13 Repeat this action twice more, but do not put lasagne sheets on the last time. Instead, cover the cheese sauce with grated cheddar.

14 Pop into the oven at 180°C and cook for about 50–60 minutes. Check at 45 minutes and if the cheese on top is going brown, cover with tin foil and return to the oven.

15 When the lasagne is ready, you will be able to put a knife through the middle easily.

16 Enjoy!

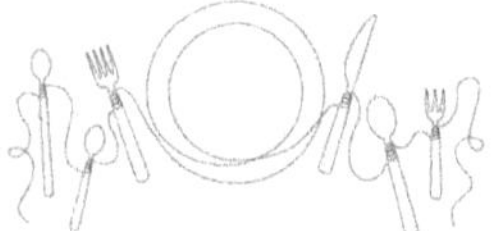

Prayer for harvest

Lord, we thank you for all you have given us. You are such a generous God, who tells us only to knock on the door and it will be opened; only to ask and it will be given. Help us, Lord, to share your love and generosity with others. Give us a generous heart, Lord, and guide us to those situations that could do with our time and gifts. Help us to see the need around us and to take the time to stop and help where we can. Let your love shine out of us as we do so. Amen.

7
Food

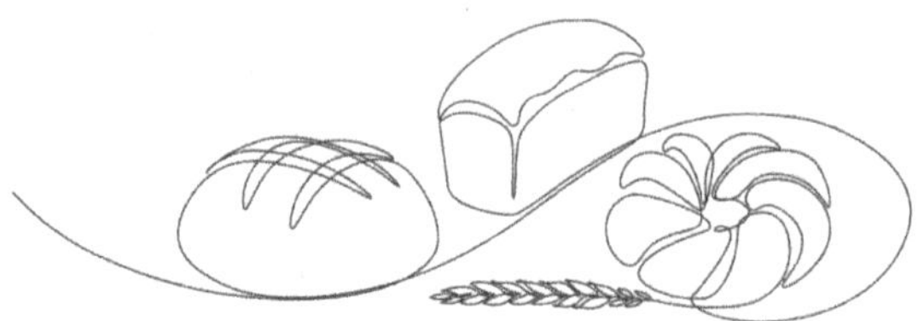

> Food cannot take care of spiritual, psychological and emotional problems, but the feeling of being loved and cared for, the actual comfort of the beauty and flavour of food, the increase of blood sugar and physical well-being, help one to go on during the next hours better equipped to meet the problems.
> (Edith Schaeffer, *The Hidden Art of Homemaking*)[10]

> Then God said, 'I give you every seed-bearing plant on the face of the whole earth and every tree that has fruit with seed in it. They will be yours for food. And to all the beasts of the earth and all the birds in the sky and all the creatures that move along the ground – everything that has the breath of life in it – I give every green plant for food.' And it was so.
> (Genesis 1:29–30)

'Eat food. Not too much. Mostly plants.' I read this sentence over and over again. It was revolutionary to me – a simple mantra that managed to sum up exactly what I had been reading elsewhere over the previous few days. It was in Michael Pollan's thought-provoking book *In Defense of Food*, where he explores the severe issues caused by our highly processed food culture. And these issues have only become worse since the book was published in 2008.

I was at university, twenty-one years old and suffering with anxiety. I was also, for the first time in my life, struggling with bad skin and other symptoms such as weight gain and insomnia. I was looking for answers beyond the medication offered by doctors. Medication has a very important place for those struggling with their mental health, but my metabolism is such that I often suffer a lot of very harsh side effects when I am taking medication, and I rarely seem to feel the benefits of the drug I am taking. I was trying to find a holistic approach to calming my nervous system and, along with a new daily movement routine, I had discovered nutrition and slow food.

Have you ever felt at a complete loss when it comes to knowing what you should be eating and when? Have you felt overwhelmed by the vast amount of health advice that bombards us on a daily basis? Or totally confused by the bright packets in supermarkets that shout things like '20% more protein'? I mean, do we even want 20% more protein in our chocolate biscuits?!

God created food and the seasons. He designed them perfectly, to feed us and to give our bodies the nourishment they need. But in this fast-paced world, we've lost our connection to real food. We've become overwhelmed by the shouts of big corporations telling us what we should eat, all competing for our attention so they can make the most money. Advertising is often focused on sugar-filled and processed foods. It's no wonder we feel confused and exhausted by it all.

What we eat matters

Processed foods make up most of the standard diet here in the UK, and they are really bad for us. I could go on and on about the effects, but I am not a scientist or a doctor. Instead, I would like to point you to a very helpful book: *Ultra-processed People* by Chris van Tulleken. I have also added some other books to the Resources page if you'd like to learn more about nutrition.

But it isn't just our bodies that are affected by the food we eat. Much of what we consume in the UK is covered in harmful pesticides and chemicals. These are not only terrible for our bodies; they are also killing the planet. We are seeing a massive decline in insect populations due to the number of pesticides used in the UK and this is having a knock-on effect for the entire ecosystem.

The rate at which we farm the land is also causing huge issues with our soil. Not only are we pumping pesticides and chemical fertilisers into it, but our consumption of food is growing at such a fast rate that the planet simply can't keep up. We are physically draining essential supplies from the land we live on and need to survive.

All this is before we get on to the issue of who works in the supply chain of our food industry. The government is acutely aware of the issues of modern slavery within our farming and agricultural industry. According to the UK Modern Slavery & Exploitation Helpline, farming and agriculture have been consistently ranked in the top five sectors for labour exploitation over the last five years. The Seasonal Worker Scheme, a scheme that addresses the lack of labour within peak times of the farming year by allowing people from abroad to come and work for the harvest season, has increased the chances of exploitation hugely. The lack of monitoring, the rural locations and the workers' limited understanding of their rights in the UK have allowed modern-day slavery to take hold within British farming.

For some items, we have got used to paying less than they cost to produce. We are bombarded with adverts telling us that this supermarket has the lowest prices, or that supermarket has price-matched or reduced or made products even cheaper. But if it seems too good to be true, it is. Someone is paying the price, always, whether that's a farmer being underpaid for goods, or workers being exploited and trafficked into modern slavery.

Slow it down

The slow-food movement has been gaining support online, much like slow living has. Slowing down with our food offers a simpler way, a better way – a way that allows us to do what is best for our bodies, our planet and our fellow humans. Jesus tells us to do two things:

> 'Love the Lord your God with all your heart and with all your soul and with all your mind and with all your strength.' The second is this: 'Love your neighbour as yourself.' There is no commandment greater than these.
> (Mark 12:30–31)

As Christians, then, it is our duty to care for our neighbours and, as with our clothes, this means voting with our purse so that the everyday things we choose to buy make a big difference in our world. Moving away from fast food, convenience and lots of cheap, plastic packaging might sound overwhelming and a lot of work, but give yourself some time and it will become a habit.

When I became unwell, one of the recommendations I found everywhere was to change my diet. Plenty of people and websites said I should move to a wholefood, organic diet with no sugar and lots of plants. At first I felt completely overwhelmed by the idea. For a number of years it just seemed like one thing too many on top of the exhausting list of things I was already unable to do due to fatigue. I had always cooked from scratch, but paring everything down to being homemade? Baking the bread we ate, whipping up pizza instead of buying it, making my own stock for soups and stews – this seemed like far too much work.

And it was. Starting to do all of it at once would have been totally insane. My poor exhausted brain would never have coped. But I decided to take it one step at a time. Learn one thing at a time. Make one thing a habit so that it doesn't feel difficult; eventually it becomes second nature.

At the time of writing this book it has been less than a year since I started my sourdough journey. Eight months to be precise. And yet it has become a part of my weekly routine. I know when to feed Betsy (my sourdough starter), when to start my loaf, the amount of flour, water, starter and salt to put together, how to shape it and how to bake it. At first I had to read a recipe, but now it is second nature. And boy has it added so much to my life! I love my sourdough routine. I love the simplicity of it, the relaxing nature of slowly forming a loaf over a few days. It means I know exactly what is for lunch every weekend because there is always a fresh loaf available.

And it isn't just me who has found this. I have a friend who, when she heard I was getting into sourdough, asked if she could take a bit of starter. She now has a weekly sourdough routine, making sure they always have a loaf of delicious home-baked bread for Sabbath.

Slowing down our food is a great way to add some 'slow' to our lives in general. Most of us eat three times a day, so cooking or preparing meals is an opportunity to take a mindful moment and focus on the present.

There are lots of studies to suggest that cooking can be a mindful and relaxing pastime. It is also an opportunity to find joy in the mundane. You might only be cooking up a simple chicken soup for dinner, but the love and care you put into the dish will make it taste all the better. It will slow you down after a long day at work and allow you to savour the simple pleasure of a good, home-cooked meal.

Make it your own

If you're reading this thinking that you really want to make changes but you're not sure where to start, then fear not! We are going to go into some very practical ways we can begin to change our eating. But before we do, I want to preface this by saying that every family is different. Everyone has different needs. The most important thing when moving to a slower way of eating is to find what works for you and your family. If making sourdough is simply too time-consuming and you don't even like bread that much anyway, then don't bother! If every now and then you really love a pre-made meal from the freezer section of the supermarket, then of course that is totally fine. You are in control here. It is important you make your food work for you.

I hope this chapter will give you some inspiration for slowing down your food, making better choices and having a positive impact on yourself and the planet. Which of these suggestions you adopt is totally up to you. Remember to take it slowly, try not to get overwhelmed and listen to your body.

Get rid of the junk

So, where do we start? A great place to begin is to get rid of the junk food. It is estimated that in the UK the average adult is consuming about two thirds of their daily calories from ultra-processed foods, or UPFs as they are known in the industry. That is totally bonkers! We need to get back to eating *real* food. Here are the ways I try to stay away from the junk.

Eating a wholefood diet

This is something that took me years to do and I am still far from perfect at it, but you know what? I'm okay with that! I slowly phased out all the junk

– the products that came in a packet or had a ton of ingredients written on them – and swapped them for a wholefood alternative. Do I still eat crisps and ice cream sometimes? Yes, of course I do! I am human! But I always try to keep it to a minimum, making sure that 80% of my diet is wholefoods, and trying to indulge with high quality, artisan or homemade treats.

So, what is a wholefood? According to the Oxford dictionary it is a 'food that has been processed or refined as little as possible and is free from additives and other artificial substances'. Basically, it is food that is as similar to its natural state as possible, like fruit, vegetables, nuts, seeds, grass-fed or free-range meat, milk, eggs and wild fish.

This is one of the easiest ways to slow down your diet. Eating natural wholefoods is great for you but also great for the planet, because a lot of the time they come in their own planet-created packaging, like a banana, apple or orange. Absolutely no need for plastic!

Of course, we can't constantly eat wholefoods. Sometimes we might want some pasta or a loaf of bread. A good trick to remember when picking a packet of food off the shelves is to check the ingredients list. If it has more than five ingredients or includes any ingredients you don't understand and wouldn't find in a household kitchen, then don't buy it. You want to pare it down as much as possible. Keep it simple. Remember: 'Eat food . . . Mostly plants.'

Eating organic

A long time ago I made the decision to eat an organic wholefoods diet. I know this isn't financially possible for everyone – and I will share some tricks on how to get the best out of your food without going organic shortly – but if you *can* afford it, I would highly recommend making the switch. There have been many studies showing a link between exposure to pesticides and an increased risk of some cancers. Research also suggests it could be the cause of many other illnesses too. I tend to find now that when I eat non-organic food for any length of time, it causes digestive issues and can make me quite unwell.

Changing to an organic diet has made a huge difference to my health and the health of my family. It has cost us more financially, but there really is nothing better to invest our money in than our health, and that starts with how we fuel our bodies. We also get the added benefit of knowing we are helping the planet by choosing food that doesn't put harmful pesticides and chemicals into the environment.

But if organic food or a totally organic diet feels too difficult or financially impossible, there is a good rule of thumb. Try to buy organic fruit and veggies that you eat the skin of, such as apples or grapes, but if it's something from which you are going to peel away a thick skin, like oranges or bananas, choose a non-organic version. This isn't a perfect resolution, and it is still possible the chemicals will have got through the skin of the food, but it's a good place to start.

If you're buying non-organic food and not removing the skin, you can also soak in a large sink of water with a tablespoon of apple cider vinegar to help wash away some of the chemicals. Make sure you give everything a good scrub!

Eating seasonally

Have you ever got to the autumn and just craved a big warming bowl of root vegetable soup? Or been desperate for a fresh leaf salad in the height of summer? God created our bodies and the food we need to nourish them. He knows exactly what we need and when we need it. The seasons are created perfectly, and so is the food that grows in them.

Eating seasonally is a great way to slow down your food, listen to your body and give it exactly what it needs. You'll also be taking care of the planet in the best way possible. But how can we do this when we shop in a normal supermarket? It is very easy: we simply look for the produce that is grown in the UK. And if it's come from just down the road, then even better! Look out for labels on fruit and veg, meat and fish, milk, cheese and so on. They will normally have info about where the food was grown and picked. You can also find a list of what's seasonal each month online, so have a search and see what you fancy.

Eating grass fed and free range

If you're a meat eater but can't afford organic meat, another great option is grass fed or free range. It will say on the packet whether your meat has been grass fed, so it's an easy one to find in supermarkets. You can also order boxes online (see below for ideas of where to buy these).

I would also highly recommend buying the best eggs you can afford and at least buying free range. Trust me, once you've had a good quality egg, you'll never be able to go back!

Where to buy

The one issue with organic food in supermarkets is that it tends to come in lots of plastic packaging and is often grown outside the UK. To counteract this, you could choose a farm box. We have had a farm box delivered to our door weekly for eight years now. Our personal favourite is Riverford Organic, but there are lots of options out there, including from farms local to you that will offer doorstep delivery. Some, like Riverford, will also include meat, dairy, eggs and cupboard staples.

Wholefood, organic delivery services have opened up a range of amazing foods many of us couldn't otherwise access. My sister-in-law regularly orders a grass-fed, free-range meat box from a farm in the UK to stock her freezer and I have ordered bulk items such as pasta and rice from low-waste shops.

Shopping online makes sustainable, high-quality food accessible to many, but if you prefer to shop in person, there are lots of great options around the UK, from farm shops to zero-waste stores, for your non-perishable cupboard staples. Some supermarkets in the UK have even started to offer a zero-waste section, where you can bring your own containers to fill with pasta, rice, beans and so on. Do a bit of research and see what you can find in your local area.

Farmers' markets are also a great option and are becoming more common. The difficulty is finding ones that don't just sell beautiful artisan products and do in fact sell groceries, but do some research and see what you can find. You might have to try a few out before you find your local vegetable stall.

Cook from scratch

This one can seem a bit overwhelming if you've never tried it before, but cooking food from scratch is a big part of getting rid of the junk. There is so much hiding in our processed foods (just look at all the ingredients on the packet!) and it can make a big difference to cook from scratch, not to mention the meditative process of cooking.

Start simple – perhaps by getting rid of that shop-bought pasta sauce and swapping it for a homemade tomato sauce (see recipe below), or you could make up a sandwich at home rather than buying a pre-made one from the shop by work. Small changes add up and soon you'll be making more and more.

Here are my top tips for making cooking from scratch easier:

- *Cook in bulk* – Don't give yourself extra work by cooking every night. I regularly make big portions of food and have the leftovers later in the week. When you've got time to cook, why not make a bolognese for eight people, giving you plenty in the freezer for a quick and easy meal. It is no extra work and means a lot less effort down the line. Just make sure you get yourself some good storage boxes and space in the freezer.
- *Use time-saving devices* – I love my slow cooker! I use it constantly. It is a great option for throwing ingredients in and leaving them all day while I work. I then get to come home to a delicious home-cooked meal and all the work has already been done. You can also make lots of portions as mentioned above! Another device I love is my soup maker. This little kitchen aid will cook and blend a delicious soup. All you have to do is add the chopped veg, some stock and press the button. Investing in some devices to help make life easier is so worth it.
- *Try a new recipe each week* – I have been cooking my own meals from scratch for over a decade now and I have a whole range of meals in my arsenal. But I didn't have a clue when I first began. This comes from years and years of trying out different recipes and learning my favourites off by heart. If you feel overwhelmed learning to cook from scratch, then choose just one recipe a week to try. Make it in bulk and fill your freezer. Eventually you'll have a whole range of dishes you can choose from, half of which you cooked beforehand!
- *Master one skill at a time* – I had always wanted to bake my own sourdough, but with everything else going on in my life it was simply one thing too many. I left it until I had the time to spend on it. If you try to master multiple cooking skills at once you will get yourself in a panic. Instead, focus on one thing. Maybe you really want to learn

how to bake sourdough, like I did. Or perhaps you want to make your own stock. Or maybe just some simple pasta sauces for the week. Whatever it is, focus on one thing at a time. Learn how to do it without concentrating or without a recipe. Once it becomes second nature your brain will be able to take on more.

Here are some simple recipes to get you started:

Simple tomato sauce

Serves 4

This is a nice simple recipe – perfect for beginners. It will give you a basic tomato pasta sauce, but feel free to add whatever you'd like. Ideal for experimenting and using up leftovers in the fridge.

Ingredients

- 1 onion
- 2 tins chopped tomatoes
- 1–2 garlic cloves, minced or crushed
- A glug of olive oil
- *Optional*: Additional ingredients of your choosing

Method

1. Finely chop the onion.
2. Heat a glug of olive oil in a flat-bottomed frying pan.
3. Fry the onions on a medium to low heat until they turn translucent.
4. Add the garlic and cook for a minute.
5. Pour in the chopped tomatoes. Leave on a low heat to simmer for 20 minutes or so.
6. Add any other ingredients you choose, such as grated cheese, fresh basil, spinach or cooked meat.

Nana's bologness

Serves 4

This is a classic recipe passed down from my nana to my mum and now to me. We have all made it our own and even my sister, who is vegan, makes it by swapping the mince for vegan mince. It's a good crowd pleaser and easy to make in bulk for the freezer or for hosting.

Ingredients

- 500 g organic/grass-fed beef mince
- 1 onion, finely chopped
- 2 garlic cloves, minced or crushed
- 200 g mushrooms, sliced
- 800 ml tinned chopped tomatoes
- 1 tbsp tomato purée
- Red wine, to taste
- Olive oil
- Salt and pepper
- Dried oregano

Method

1 Heat a small amount of olive oil in a large saucepan with a lid. Once hot, add the mince and stir until browned.
2 Add the onion and cook until translucent.
3 Add the mushrooms and cook until softened.
4 Add the garlic and cook for about a minute.
5 Pour in the chopped tomatoes and bring up to temperature.
6 Add red wine, to taste (I like quite a lot!).
7 Add the tomato purée, dried oregano, salt and pepper, then stir.

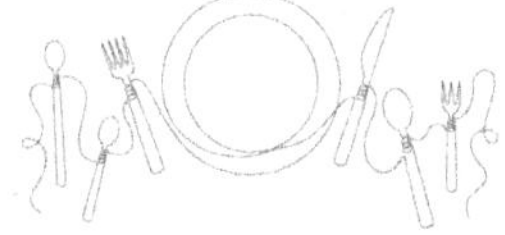

8 Turn the heat right down and leave to cook on the hob for about an hour. Keep stirring every so often and if there is still a lot of liquid, leave the lid off for the last 15 minutes. You can also add more tomato purée if thickening is required.
9 Serve on top of pasta.

Mum's quiche

Serves 6–8

My mum's quiche is legendary. It is loved by all who get to have a slice – and that has been quite a lot of people over the years! Quiche is such a simple dish and works well as one to give away, as it can be eaten cold or easily heated up. You can also adapt the ingredients to make it work for individual tastes and requirements. Here I am sharing one of my favourite flavour combos: chorizo and red pepper.

Ingredients

- 400 g plain flour
- 200 g butter, cut into 1 cm cubes
- 4 medium eggs
- 2 egg yolks
- 350–400 ml milk
- 200 g cheddar cheese, grated
- 1 red pepper, cut into slices
- 150 g chorizo sausage, cut into small chunks

Method

1. Preheat the oven to 200°C/180°C fan/gas 6 and grease a flan dish (I like to use a ceramic one to make cutting into the quiche easier after cooking).
2. In a large bowl, rub the cubed butter into the flour using your thumb against your fingers. Continue until you have a fine breadcrumb consistency.
3. Add a small amount of water and use a flat knife to combine the breadcrumb mix with the water. Keep adding water and mixing until you have a dough.
4. Roll out the dough onto a floured surface, about 0.5

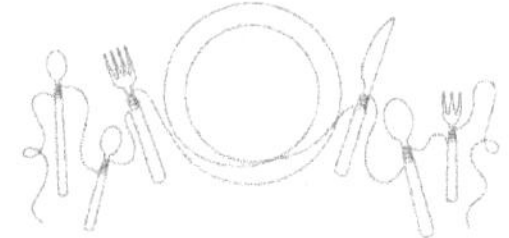

cm thick. Using the rolling pin, lift the dough onto the greased flan dish and gently push into the edges.

5 Once the pastry is sitting nicely in the dish, trim any excess around the sides with a knife, leaving a little more pastry than you want, as it will shrink during cooking.

6 Fry the chorizo and peppers together until cooked. You shouldn't need any oil as the chorizo will release a lot.

7 Once cooked, pour the chorizo and pepper mix on top of the pastry base and spread out evenly. You can use a slotted spoon to stop too much chorizo oil getting into the quiche, but personally I think this gives the quiche a great flavour.

8 Beat the eggs and egg yolks together. Add the milk and beat this in.

9 Add a little salt and pepper, then pour the egg mix carefully on top of the chorizo and pepper. The mix will move around as the egg comes in, so do it gently to try to keep an even spread of the filling.

10 Add the grated cheddar a bit at a time, pressing it into the quiche as you go. This can get a bit messy, but it is better to mix the cheese into the egg rather than having it all on top.

11 Bake in the oven for about 25 minutes until golden brown on top. If you're planning to give this away to someone who is going to heat it up themselves, cook for 20 minutes so they can brown it up.

12 When reheating from chilled, pop into an oven at 200°C/180°C fan/gas 6, covered in tin foil for 15 minutes and uncovered for the last 5 minutes.

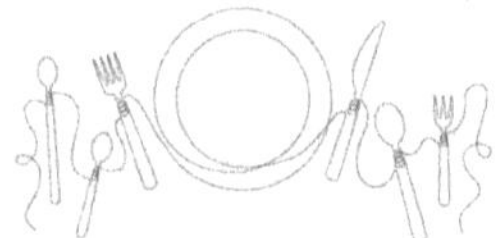

Bake your own sourdough

Is there anything better than the smell of bread baking in the oven? Or the sound of a fresh crust as you slowly cut a slice? I love making bread and as I've mentioned before, one of my favourites is sourdough. Many of us got into bread-making during the Covid lockdowns because it is a beautifully rhythmic and engaging activity. All in all, it takes about thirty-six hours to make a loaf of sourdough, and that process can really help us to slow right down and stay in the present moment. Back then, it offered a sense of stability and calm away from what felt like quite a frightening world for many of us.

Making sourdough is a uniquely communal baking task, with many of us gifting or receiving sourdough starters. You can make your own, but I do love the communal nature of passing on the starter!

So, what exactly is sourdough and why is it so great? Sourdough is a fermented dough made using a sourdough starter instead of yeast. The starter is a living culture that helps the dough to rise much like yeast does. A sourdough starter is a natural leavening agent and one we would have used before packet yeast was invented.

But sourdough is more than just a natural and slow way to leaven your bread. As the grains in the dough ferment during the long process of baking a loaf, the enzymes in the wheat begin to break down, meaning the bread becomes lower in gluten, making it much easier for your body to digest. The fermented grains are also a great boost to gut health.

Your starter

I would always recommend trying to get a starter from someone else or ordering one off the internet. You can make your own, but it is quite a complicated process and when you're starting your baking journey, it is better to find a starter that is nice and active.

Once you have your starter you need to feed it. Simply weigh out your starter and add the same weight in strong white bread flour and lukewarm water. Mix together, put in a jar with a sealed lid and leave in a warm place to become active. Make sure the contents of your jar have room to grow. I never fill my starter jars more than half way. This might leave you with some discard. There are tons of discard recipes online and I have included my favourite website for sourdough recipes on the Resources page.

It should take between twelve and fifteen hours for your starter to become active. You will know when it's happened, because it will have doubled in size and become very bubbly.

How often you feed your starter depends on how often you want to use it. I bake a loaf of bread and some other things like pizza dough and flatbreads once a week. I do a bulk baking day and freeze food for later. This means I feed my starter only once a week. The rest of the time it lives in the fridge. If you want to activate it only once a week, you *must* keep it in the fridge, or it will go off. And to keep your starter healthy you should feed it at least once a week, whether you use it to bake or not.

If you are baking something with your starter every day, or every other day, you can leave it out at room temperature and feed it every twenty-four hours.

A simple loaf recipe

There are lots of ways to make sourdough and I am very much still learning, but this is my go-to loaf recipe:

Ingredients

- 275 g strong white bread flour
- 200 g mixed grain bread flour
- 100 g active sourdough starter
- 350 ml lukewarm water
- 2 tsp sea salt flakes

Equipment

- Large mixing bowl
- Beeswax wrap, or plate large enough to cover the bowl
- Banneton basket (a special basket used for proofing sourdough)
- Muslin cloth or tea towel
- Cast-iron pot with lid

Method

1. Mix the water and active sourdough starter together.
2. Mix the flours together in the bowl, then pour the water and starter mix on top. Using a spoon or your hands, bring it all together to form a dough.
3. Cover the bowl with the beeswax wrap or plate. Leave to rest at room temperature for about 30 minutes.
4. Uncover the dough and sprinkle the salt evenly over it. Use your fingers to prod it into the dough, making sure it is well incorporated. Cover and leave for another 30 minutes.
5. Perform a series of stretch-and-folds: take the side of the dough and pull it upwards, stretching it out gently, being

careful not to tear it, and then place this back down in the middle. Give the bowl a quarter turn and repeat the action three times.

6 Cover and leave in a warm place.
7 Repeat steps 5 and 6 five more times, or until the dough is looking shiny and is starting to feel springy.
8 Cover the bowl and leave in a warm place for 7–8 hours. The timing will depend on how warm your home is. You want the dough to double in size and have some bubbles.
9 Once the dough is fermented enough, pour it out onto a floured work surface. Pull the sides gently with your hands until it becomes a rough rectangle. Fold the sides in so it forms a long rectangle, then bring the top and bottom (the short ends of the rectangle) in one at a time, so it forms a slightly square dome shape.
10 Now push and pull the dough to form it into a ball and create structure. This technique can take time to learn, and I recommend using a YouTube video to see the technique. Make sure you have plenty of flour to stop the dough from sticking.
11 Once you feel the dough has formed a good round shape and has some structure to it, place in a floured banneton basket and cover with a muslin cloth. Leave in the fridge over night for its final fermentation.
12 The next day, heat your oven to 255°C/250°C fan, then place your cast-iron pot inside to heat up for 45–60 minutes.
13 Once your pot is hot, tip your cold dough out onto a piece of baking paper. This is the point at which you can score it with pretty designs, but make sure you at least do one deep score either across the dough or in a semi-circle to the side.

14 Pick up the baking paper and carefully slide it inside the hot cast-iron pot, placing the lid on top.
15 Cook in the oven with the lid on for 25 minutes, then turn the oven down to 245°C/240°C fan/gas 9 and take the lid off. Leave to cook for another 20 minutes.
16 Take the bread out of the oven, carefully lifting it from the pot using the paper, and leave to cool on a rack.
17 Enjoy your delicious sourdough loaf!

Forage

Foraging is another great option for getting hold of organic wholefoods that are amazing for your body and it's also free (yes, free!). This is something we have started doing more and more since moving to the countryside, but you don't have to live next to fields to enjoy it. Foraging is available in a lot of places, even in the city if you know where to look! Here are some ideas on how to get started:

- *Buy yourself a good guide* – This is really important, because you want to always be 100% sure of what you're picking. *Never* pick anything you aren't sure about and always double check. Guides will also help you to know what to look for in each season and where to look. You might even find a guide for your local area.
- *Join a group* – Foraging groups are popping up all over the UK and are a great option for the novice forager, or the seasoned forager who fancies making some like-minded friends to go foraging with. You can learn so much from others and it's always very helpful to have someone to double check your finds.
- *Look out for a good spot* – I am always on the hunt throughout the year for good foraging spots. I will note down a place where the hedgerows look full of brambles ready for blackberries later in the autumn, or take notice of a woodland area that looks as though it could be a good option for wild garlic in the spring. Keep a note of the places you see throughout the year and make your way back to them at the right time.
- *Pick sparingly and tread lightly* – The most important rule in foraging, other than being 100% sure of what you are picking, is to pick only a little at a time. Leave some for nature. If you take all the leaves off a wild garlic plant, it will die and not be there next year for you or others. It is very important to respect the nature you are picking from, to share with the wildlife and to allow the plants to continue to thrive. See below for some more specifics on picking certain foods.

When you're first starting off, it's a good idea to stick to the foods that are plentiful and easy to spot and identify. This way you can enjoy the process of foraging wild foods and start to learn a bit about becoming a responsible forager. Here are some easy plants to pick throughout the seasons:

Spring

Nettles are one of the easiest plants to identify. We all know what stinging nettles look like – and feel like when we aren't careful around them! But what a lot of people don't know is that they are actually an amazing source of iron, zinc, magnesium, selenium, potassium and vitamins A and C. They are also a fantastic treatment for post-partum bleeding and can help with the production of breast milk. Many women also find nettles to be useful during their period, as they can help lighten heavy periods and replenish the body with iron. And don't worry – once they are cooked or dried they don't sting!

It is best to pick nettles when they are young and fresh. March is about the right time to do it. Try to pick from a patch away from the road and a little distance from the path. You will need to wear gloves and long sleeves, and bring some sort of container and scissors with you for harvesting. Take the very top of the nettle plant, about 15 centimetres, with three to five leaves. Make sure the plant is at a height that means it should be free of dog wee! Once the nettles have got flowers and seeds on them, they are too far over and will have become very bitter in flavour, so pick only the fresh plants. Once you get them home, give them a good wash.

You can use nettles in the same way you use cooked spinach. They are delicious in stews, soups and currys. The other option is to leave them out to dry. You can do this by hanging them in a warm dry area for a few weeks or laying them out on a tray. Once dried they can be ground into a powder to put into smoothies (a real super-food!) or you can make your own nettle tea by placing a handful of dried leaves in a tea pot and adding hot water. Leave them to steep for fifteen minutes. Drinking nettle tea can be helpful during your period or post-partum.

Wild garlic has become a popular foraging delight in recent years. It grows close to the ground in woodland spaces and has long arrow-shaped leaves. But the easiest way to identify it is to smell it. It should smell garlicky! Depending on where you are in the country, you can pick wild garlic from the end of March until the beginning of May. Once the plants begin to flower they become bitter and are best left, but the sight of a forest floor covered in tiny white wild garlic flowers, along with the incredible smell, is worth a walk.

Sadly, we have seen some very irresponsible picking in the last few years, resulting in wild garlic spots being absolutely decimated. These are places where wild garlic has grown for years and years and may never recover, so *please* pick responsibly. You should only pick one or two leaves from each plant so that it can still photosynthesise. The whole wonderful point of foraging is to enjoy seasonal delights. You shouldn't be picking enough to last all year but just enough to make a few seasonal treats.

You can use this herb in any dishes that suit garlic. Simply chop up finely and enjoy. Personally, I like to make garlic butter to spread on cheese scones and put into mushroom risotto.

Garlic butter recipe

Ingredients

- 250 g butter
- 100 g wild garlic, washed and finely chopped
- Pinch of sea salt flakes

Method

1. Leave the butter out at room temperature to soften.
2. Once soft enough, place the butter into a mixing bowl and mash with a fork.
3. Add the wild garlic and salt, stirring until thoroughly combined.
4. Spoon the garlic butter mix out onto some baking paper about 5 cm from the bottom. Try to create a rough sausage shape.
5. Roll the butter sausage up in the paper, twisting the ends so that it looks like a cracker, then pop into the freezer.
6. We like to keep ours in the freezer and chop chunks of it off to use for different meals. It will last for about 3 months in the freezer or a couple of weeks in the fridge.

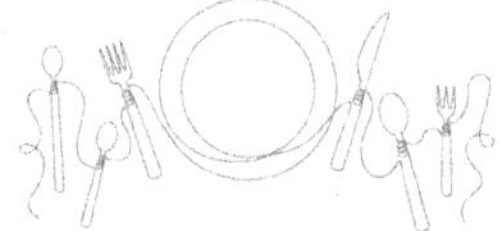

Summer

Elderflower is truly the taste of summer and is such a wonderful plant to forage. I just love the time towards the end of May, when the countryside begins to deck itself out in white, and the elder trees throw out their frothy lace umbrella of cream flowers.

Elderflower grows on elder trees, which are easy to spot. They will be covered in cloudy white flowers that smell incredible and form an umbrella shape. The leaves grow in sets of five and are arrow-shaped. Cut the whole flower umbrella when harvesting, but again don't take too much. We want the plant to thrive and to bring us lots of berries in the autumn.

Once home, give the flowers a delicate wash and shake off any little bugs and beasties. Cut the flowers off, snipping close to the heads as the stems are faintly toxic.

Elderflower has all sorts of uses, but a lot of people enjoy it in cordial. I am not the biggest fan of a simple floral drink, so I love to mix mine with rhubarb, which is seasonal at this time, for a floral but sharp cordial that is delightful with sparkling water.

Blackberries begin in late summer and I absolutely love blackberry season, watching the juicy fruit turn from bright lime green to pink to jewel red and then finally to deep dark purply black. They make great little snacks for walks with kids and dogs, and are a very prolific fruit, so you can collect them over a few weeks and fill your freezer for later in the year. Try to find a patch away from the road so as to avoid pollution, and high up from the ground to avoid dog wee!

You can tell the fruit is ready to be picked when it comes away easily but doesn't completely squish in your fingers (then it is too far over). Collect a good bowlful and bring them home to wash thoroughly. You can then make jams, jellies, cakes, crumbles and many other delicious dishes, or you can pop them in the freezer for later in the year. I like to do a mix of both. There's nothing better than an apple and blackberry cake in the cold depths of winter to bring back a taste of sun-kissed berries and late summer.

Autumn/winter

Elderberries are the berries formed by the same plant as the elderflower we picked in the summer – those flowers you left on the tree. They are now delicious dark purple berries with incredible health-boosting benefits. They are good for the immune system due to their antiviral and anti-allergy effects, and they are an amazing source of vitamins A and C.

Elderberries are easy to spot. Look out for the elder tree again and you'll find that the umbrella stems have now turned bright pinky red, and instead of flowers, they are laden down with tiny dark berries. Once again you should cut the whole umbrella but make sure you leave the plant with some berries for the birds and other wildlife.

Once home, give them a really good wash and cut the berries off close to the stem (these are still faintly toxic). You can then use the berries to make cordial or syrup, which served with hot water in the winter can be the much-needed tonic for your body to stay well or fend off a cold. You can also make delicious sauces, sorbets and puddings.

Rosehips are another great wild food, perfect for the coming winter season and filled with vitamin C for staving off flu and colds. (It is almost as if God knew exactly what we needed and when …) They are the berries left on rose plants and are normally ready to pick after the first frost, so about November time, depending on where you live in the UK.

You can pick rosehips from any rose plant – all roses are safe to eat – but I tend to go out to the hedgerows and pick from the dog-rose plants. You simply pull the heads off. They should be bright red like little jewels, a long oval shape and firm but not hard if they are ready to be picked. Watch out for thorns on the rose plants.

Give them a good wash when you get home, then top and tail them. Rosehips cannot be eaten raw; they are bit tough and don't taste like much, so will need quite a bit of preparation. You can use them for an immunity-boosting syrup to drink with hot water in the winter, or poured over puddings. You can also make jams and jellies with them (search online for recipes).

Sloes are great too for foraging as we go from autumn into winter. Again, it is said that the best time to gather them is after the first frost. They are thought to contain a high level of antioxidants, but they will lose some of their nutrients when preserved. Like the rosehip, you cannot eat these raw and they will need to be put into something.

Sloes grow on blackthorn bushes and are dark bluey-black berries. They are easy to identify due to their colour and the way they grow in clusters around the branch, with small green leaves around them. Make sure you wash them thoroughly once you get them home.

A firm favourite use of sloes in the UK is as an infusion for gin. This gives the gin a deep berry flavour and if started in November can usually be ready for a Christmas treat! Other options are hedgerow jam or jelly, or a sauce for pork.

However you buy, prepare and eat your food, slowing down is such a wonderful way to savour the everyday and remind yourself of the blessings God has given you. Food is one of God's great gifts and should never be rushed but enjoyed. Spend time meditatively preparing meals, blessing your family and friends with them and joining in community as you enjoy them together.

8
Home

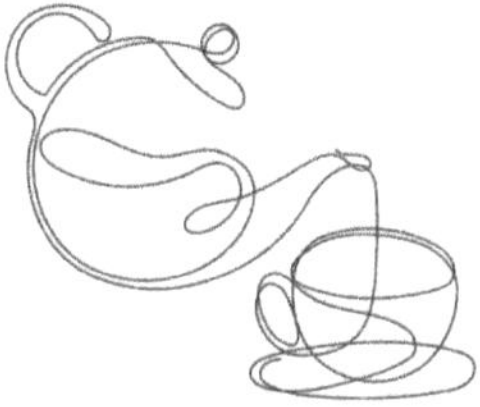

> Have nothing in your house that you do not know to be useful or believe to be beautiful.
> (William Morris, 1834–96)

> But as for me and my household, we will serve the LORD.
> (Joshua 24:15)

It wasn't long ago that the home was the centre of the family, where people gathered together daily and where all of life happened at kitchen tables and in rocking chairs in front of the fire. Men would go out to work, but women and children stayed and worked within the home. If you were lucky enough to be working your own land, then as a man you would return throughout the day to eat and rest, then go and work some more. The home would be a sanctuary, a quiet and warm space away from the world, and it is still one of the most important things for us as humans.

When God placed Adam and Eve in the garden, he was giving them a home, a safe space in which to dwell in communion with him. He gave them work and tasks. They were to keep the garden in which they lived beautiful, as God had made it. And throughout history, ever since Adam and Eve were forced to leave Eden, their home, the whole human race has been trying to find home again.

As Christians we know that it isn't possible to find our true home on this earth. We are destined for a new life, somewhere else. But until that day comes, we search for a feeling of home, a place to belong here on the earth God created. And that comes when we are in relationship with God our Father. That sense of belonging and safety is real when we live in communion with him.

So how can the homes we live in reflect this? And why is that an important part of living a slow and simple life for God?

God the designer

God is the ultimate creator and designer. He made the inky black of a night sky sparkling with stars, the unfurling of peony petals in the June sunshine and the bright red of a robin's breast. No one can do it better than God. He made our home here on this earth beautiful, because he knew how important it was. There have been many studies to show the positive health benefits of looking at beautiful things – from flowers in the home actively lifting our mood to that sense of awe when we look at a stunning view, calming our nervous system and keeping us in the present moment.

Last year I was lucky enough to go to the alpine town of Füssen in Germany. We visited Neuschwanstein Castle and climbed to the viewing balcony. I had never seen anything like it. It felt as though the whole of the Alps had been put on display just for us. The sky was a bright china blue, white snow was painted across craggy mountains that seemed to go on for miles and a frozen blue lake sat at the bottom. I was in total awe of God's design, feeling all at once tiny but so overwhelmed that the Creator of mountains knew me by name and could count every hair on my head.

If God can adorn the world with such beauty, why should we not do the same with our homes? The spaces we curate and call home give us a unique opportunity to show God's love and creativity. Making them beautiful can be a part of our ministry for both our family and others.

When I was a newly married woman living in Oxford, I once visited the home of our minister. I had gone to have a chat with the minister's wife about something quite difficult. It was going to be a painful conversation. I remember the feeling of trepidation as I stood on the doorstep with my husband. From the outside it looked like a typical 1920s semi-detached house – nice, but nothing to report home about. The kind of house many people live in. But stepping through the door I was greeted by something so unexpected. Her home was beautiful! I felt as though I had walked into a house in Scandinavia – classic, so well executed but soft and cosy. It oozed hygge (see below). There was a fire going in the log burner and she had dimmed the lights to a soft glow. We sat on a comfy sofa and already I felt more at ease about having this conversation. It was still a hard chat, but the soft, comforting and safe environment made all the difference.

Your home matters

Our home is a powerful place. As Christians it should be a place where we serve the Lord and commune with him. A place of sanctuary and safety for the family we raise in it and those we invite into it. We are called to be generous with all we have and that includes our home. Hospitality is a fundamental part of the Christian faith, and curating a beautiful and slow home can help us in that mission.

Too often these days the home is purely somewhere to sleep. I have been horrified to read about the new pods that are being created in other countries, where most of the day is spent at work. You shower at work, eat out and only need somewhere to sleep at night, so a simple bunk bed will do. We are living life at such a fast pace that we have lost all connection to the home and why it is important. Our homes should be more than a place where we just crash out and watch Netflix in our PJs.

A home is a prayer space, a church, a school room, a rest place, a sanctuary, a safe place, a space for celebrations and a place for mourning. The home is where life happens; where church continues every day after Sunday morning, and God's work gets done. Kingdom conversations happen across the dinner table and on sofas in front of the fire and in gardens or on balconies. World-changing prayer happens in the bedroom, in the bathroom, in the living room and at the dining table. Our homes matter.

Hygge

Hygge noun: Esp. with reference to Danish culture: a quality of cosiness and comfortable conviviality that engenders a feeling of

> contentment or well-being; contentment from simple pleasures, such as warmth, food, friends, etc.
> (*Oxford Dictionary*)

Chances are you've heard of hygge (pronounced hyoo-guh). It has been a bit of a buzzword for quite a number of years now, with the cosy Nordic lifestyle becoming ever more popular. But it is quite a difficult thing to describe and we don't have a literal translation for it within our English vocabulary. I feel this speaks volumes about what different cultures value.

Hygge is essentially about well-being, being content with the simple pleasures of life and enjoying the cosiness of winter. It has developed in the Nordic countries due to their long winters with little to no daylight at some points in the year. Nordic people are forced into their homes by the weather and the light, so they have learned to make the most of it. To cosy up. To enjoy the time spent together and to find joy and light when it's dark and cold.

I have been a big fan of hygge for a while and I think that creating a hygge home can be a wonderful opportunity to make a safe, quiet, slow space away from the world, where you and others can find the rest you need. In her book *Holy Hygge: Creating a place for people to gather and the gospel to grow,* Jamie Erickson says this: 'Hygge is simple but sophisticated, warm and inviting, homemade and rustic. Hygge is the opposite of hustle. It eschews over-abundance. It savours. It takes thing slow and envelops you in sanctuary. Hygge is home.'[11]

Doesn't that sound wonderful? To slow our homes down enough to be able to savour the simple comforts and joys of life. To create a home with our hands that we feel so ourselves in and love to bring others into. This chapter isn't about creating the perfect home ready for a magazine shoot. We aren't trying to emulate Martha Stewart (although if that is your thing, then go for it!). There is no such thing as perfection on this earth, but we can work towards creating homes that encourage us to slow down and find sanctuary both for ourselves and others.

Slowing it down

How do we start making cosy, simple and slow homes that matter and praise God? You may have guessed it by now, but I am going to suggest you start by slowing down (revolutionary, I know). If our homes are going to become useful spaces for kingdom work, we actually have to slow down enough to be in them. I hope that the other chapters in this book have helped you to slow down and simplify your life, and perhaps you are already spending more time at home. But if you still feel rushed off your feet and as though you only seem to come home to sleep, I encourage you to think about this and try to work out how you might be able to spend more time in your home to recharge and rest.

Our homes should be a sanctuary where we can come away from the world and recharge in God's presence. This will help us to regain the energy to go back out and do the work God has given us, whatever that may be. I know this can be more challenging for the homemaker. Your work is the home, so it isn't quite as easy as it might be for those working outside, but it is still possible to make your home a safe place where you can rest and recharge. I hope you find some of these suggestions helpful for creating a sanctuary that works for you.

Making a beautiful home

Like everything in our lives at the moment, the level of consumption when it comes to homeware has definitely got out of control. Social media is filled with people buying houses, totally renovating them in three months and then moving in and changing all the décor at the drop of a hat. It's impossible to keep up and often leaves us feeling as though our homes are severely lacking.

Creating a beautiful space doesn't have to be expensive, time-consuming or exhausting. You can take it at your own pace. We bought our first home in our mid-twenties and worked on it little by little. Every year we improved it with painting, decorating, buying second-hand furniture, sewing blinds and growing new plants in the garden. It was a constant project, but I liked that. We took our time to work out what was right and what we wanted. And we also did it to a budget we could actually afford.

Here are my top tips for creating a beautiful home that works for you and doesn't cost a fortune or the earth.

Live in it before making big decisions

Most of us can't afford to totally redecorate a home before moving in, so living with it is par for the course. But it can actually be a very helpful way of getting to know what you do and don't need. It can be tempting when moving into a new place to get excited and spend an afternoon running round Ikea, but waiting to see what would work best for you in the space is going to help you save money and consume less. Get to know your rooms, figure out what you want to do with them and how you want to use them, and only then start your furniture shopping.

Find your style

My husband is great at interior design, but I am much less gifted. I struggle to visualise what a room could look like, so Pinterest has become my best friend. When creating a beautiful and slow home, it is essential to find your style and what you like. Similar to finding your style when it comes to clothes (see Chapter 4), you don't want to buy things on impulse without really knowing whether they will or won't work in your house. So spend some time looking at magazines, creating Pinterest boards and saving pictures on social media to get a good idea of the style of home you would like to create. You could even go super-'old school' and create some tangible mood boards with cut-outs from magazines. (You can find my Pinterest home boards on the Resources page.) There are so many different styles, but find something that brings you joy every day and makes you feel safe, cosy and content, as these are the most important things when it comes to creating a slow and satisfying home.

For me this comes from an English country cottage style. I love big comfortable sofas covered in handmade scatter cushions, old-fashioned wooden floors and big rugs thrown over them to keep toes warm. I find so much joy in a log burner, brass pans hanging in the kitchen and muddy wellies lined up by the front door.

For you it might be the hygge Scandi style that brings the most joy. Or bright colours and patterns that make you smile each day. Once you start looking at inspirational pictures you will begin to notice what lights you up, what makes you excited and what you'd like to have in your own home.

There is no right or wrong way to decorate your home. As long as it brings you joy, gives you space to relax and find sanctuary from the world and is somewhere you feel you can connect with God and invite people into, that is all that matters.

Take it one room at a time

It can be very overwhelming creating a beautiful space that you love, so I recommend trying to take it one room at a time. I know this isn't always possible, especially when buying second-hand furniture and you find pieces you absolutely cannot leave behind (like my mother-in-law, who once drove home with three passengers sitting with chairs on top of them), but slowing down and taking one step at a time can really help you get it right and enjoy the process.

Thrift your home

There is so much stuff in the world, there is little need to buy new. Not only is this a great way of saving money and the planet's resources, but you can also find the most unique and interesting pieces. It is so easy to shop for second-hand furniture now, with large charity shops in the UK such as the Salvation Army, British Heart Foundation and Oxfam superstores all open throughout the week up and down the country and often offering a delivery service. That's not to mention sources like Facebook Marketplace, Gumtree, eBay and Vinterior. You can also find smaller items such as cushions, blankets, quilts and prints on Vinted.

Charity shops will always be my favourite places to go for ornaments, beautiful crockery, glasswear, soft furnishings and so much more. You will have to root around a bit more, but that is all part of the fun. Trust me, there is no better feeling than finding an absolute gem of a piece to add unique style to your home. One top tip is to make sure you keep a list of items you could do with – on your phone or somewhere else you won't lose it. That way, when you're out and about doing some thrifting you can consult your list and remind yourself of the particular item you need. I can't tell you the number of times I have totally forgotten we need X, Y and Z only to check my phone and then see it in the next charity shop!

A handmade home

Making things for your home is a slow and beautiful process. Over the years I have made blinds, curtains, knitted blankets and cushions, and I have recently begun to quilt and embroider. There is nothing more lovely than seeing your hard work out on display in your home. And you can make it exactly to specification, choosing the style you want. You can also use sustainable materials. Of the things I've made, one of my favourites is the cushion I knitted using wool from sheep that lived near the first home we owned. We are moving on from there soon, but the cushion will be coming with us and will always be a memory of the time we spent in that part of the country and of our first ever home.

You can also source materials second hand from charity shops and online. Second-hand curtains can be cut up and reused to make new curtains or a blind that fits your window correctly. They can also be used for cushion covers, seat pads, drawstring bags and so much more, and I love second-hand bedsheets for making scatter cushions.

Don't be put off if you're totally new to making things. There are so many easy ways to learn new skills, you will be handmaking your entire home by the end of next year! YouTube is my favourite go-to for learning new handmade skills, but if you're willing to pay a little you can get subscriptions to amazing websites such as SkillShare and Create Academy, where industry experts will take you through classes in everything from curtain-making to re-upholstering an armchair, and even woodwork and furniture design.

If you prefer to learn face to face, check out your local college or craft shop for workshops and courses. There are so many options for learning new skills and making your dream home on a budget. Here are a few ideas for items you could make and projects you could tackle at home:

- Ruffle cushion
- Curtains and blinds
- Knitted/crocheted blanket or cushion
- Reupholster an old armchair or sew a slipcover
- Quilt for the bed or to use as a wall-hanging
- Rag or braided rug
- Macramé plant hangers
- Crocheted placemats or bathmat
- Upcycle old frames from the charity shop with paint samples

- Draw your own calligraphy Bible verses to frame and put on the walls

Keep it simple

Creating a simple home that isn't too busy or filled with too much stuff can be really helpful when it comes to taking care of it. Don't give yourself another set of time-consuming jobs. Create a home that feels manageable. Less stuff means less to clean and put away! I am by no means a minimalist, but we are very careful not to have anything in the house that isn't beautiful or useful. We consider everything we bring into it and don't keep homeware we no longer have a use for, just for the sake of it.

Choose pieces for your home that will help you to take care of it easily. For example, a giant chest in the living room can be used as a coffee table, but will also provide somewhere to store the children's toys at the end of the day. Clever and easy storage solutions can mean the world of difference in a busy home and make you love your space so much more.

I quite like the meditative process of making a bed and placing all the throw cushions on it each day, but if this will just frustrate you, don't have any! It's your home, and there are no rules. You're allowed to do it just the way you want to. However you decide to decorate your home, make it a space that feels like you. A home should be comfortable, safe and relaxing; a sanctuary away from the world, where you can connect with friends, family and, most importantly, God.

Working from home

If you work from home, it can be hard to find that necessary separation between home and work life. My top tip for achieving this sense of balance is to create a workstation. If you're lucky enough to have a spare bedroom you can use as an office, this is ideal, as you can shut the door on it at the end of your working day, enjoying the rest of the house as a place of sanctuary. If you don't have a dedicated office space, try adding a small table or desk somewhere in your living space. If you are able to fit this into a corner that can be forgotten about once you've finished work, that's even better. Try to avoid working from bed or the sofa if you can, otherwise these places can become associated with work rather than rest.

Rhythms and rituals can also be a helpful way to create separation from work at the end of your day. Perhaps switch off the overhead light and have lamps on. Or maybe light a candle, tidy your work stuff away and pop some music on. You could have a special pair of slippers, a blanket you like to get out or a certain mug you use to mark your finish time. Try to find a way to signal to your body that it is the end of the working day and now time to relax and reset. The home environment is moving from work space to rest space.

Hospitality

In Romans 12:13 we are told: 'Share with the Lord's people who are in need. Practise hospitality.' As Christians we are called repeatedly to be hospitable; to open our homes to others and to give generously. This is one of the beautiful things about being a part of God's family. No matter where you have come from, you can bet you'll find a warm welcome from God's people wherever you are. My husband and I have moved around a little bit and every first Sunday in a new church we have been invited back for lunch or for dinner later in the week. It is a beautiful part of church life and one that I love.

But the hospitality doesn't stop there. Most of the Christians I know are willing to open up their homes, their kitchens, their living rooms and their spare bedrooms to those who need them. It is a part of our identity, so it is really important that we don't get too bogged down with whether or not our home is 'guest ready'. Yes, it can be lovely to prepare a delicious three-course meal, make up the spare room just right with folded towels and flowers (I am a big believer in making my home into a place where I can bless people, even if that's just going to the effort of primping the spare room), but don't let that be a barrier for you. Invite people round, even if the meal isn't that fancy and you're just rustling up something out of the cupboards. Have people to stay, even if all you can manage is some clean bedding and a quick whip around the bathroom.

Don't wait for the perfect home, the perfect meal or the perfect time to host because, believe me, it will never come. There will always be something to do! I love to make my home beautiful, and I love to create delicious meals that bless those who come into my home, but neither of these is essential. If all I can rustle up is a pasta bake, then a pasta bake it will be. It is the people who matter – the conversations, the gathering together, the laughter, the tears and the communion. As in every area of life, we can allow ourselves to be whizzed up into a frenzy of too fast and too busy, focusing on the wrong things. 'If I just get one more ruffle cushion made, I can have guests to stay,' we say. Or, 'If I can just perfect this casserole, I can invite others for dinner.' It is good to strive to do our best and to find joy in creating beautiful things, but we mustn't let the focus shift too much towards this. Instead we trust the one who delights in our efforts, however small.

A house becomes a home, not because of the perfect décor or the most amazing meal plan, but because of the love and care it exudes. A home is somewhere where we are content in what God has given us, and we share it as best we can.

FESTIVE SEASON

Dark early mornings,
feet tucked into cosy socks placed gently on steps,
twinkling lights adorn trees in the corners,
hands dip into the day's pocket,
a little treat held and enjoyed,
another day ticked off,
a reminder of all that is to come,
O come, O come, Emmanuel.

Seasonal celebrations: Advent

> The weary world rejoices, for yonder breaks a new and glorious morn.
> (Placide Cappeau, 'O Holy Night', 1847)

The word 'advent' comes from the Latin word *adventus*, which means 'coming' or 'arrival'. It signals expectation. A waiting for something to happen. This is a beautiful time of year. A time to be quiet, to listen as though to the drip, drip, drip of snow as it silently falls outside.

The King is coming.

Advent is a time of expectation: we are waiting for Jesus to come. To remember the first time he came to earth as a baby, as our Saviour, and to look forward to the time when he will come again. When all pain and sorrow will cease, every tear will be wiped away and this world will be made new. 'The light shines in the darkness, and the darkness has not overcome it' (John 1:5).

A slow Advent

I love this time of year. I am a true Christmas girl. Always have been and always will be. I will start the anticipation of Christmas as early as I can. But what I want to push back against is all the rushing of it. Christmas, with its bright electric lights, non-stop churning out of old Christmas hits and constant advertisements for the perfect present can be totally overwhelming. I think you'll be able to guess by now that I propose we do Christmas slowly and simply; that we reconnect with the handmade and the homegrown, notice the beauty all around us and remind ourselves what Christmas is really all about. And a slow Christmas begins with a slow Advent.

How, then, do we calm it all down and focus on the true reason for the season? Here are some ideas to help you have a beautiful advent.

Advent study

My first tip would be to pick an Advent Bible study. It doesn't have to be a formal Bible study guide; it could be a study on an app, online or a book you read through during the month. There are so many great resources available to us now. Personally, I love to give myself the treat of going to my local Christian bookshop and having a good old browse. This works online too if you haven't got a local shop. Pick something you're excited to dig into and learn more about God this season.

Once you've got your beautiful Advent book or study, make time each day to read through it. I know it can be very busy at this time of year, but you'll never regret taking ten minutes to ground yourself in the promises of God. I love my quiet Advent mornings before the busy workday ahead. A reminder of Emmanuel; that God is with us.

Alternative Advent calendars

I love an Advent calendar! A tiny little treat each day for twenty-four days in the lead-up to a day full of celebration? Yes, please – thank you very much! But these days Advent calendars often come filled with plastic, much of which can't be recycled, and bearing chocolate with a dubious supply chain.

If you're all about the chocolate, there are lots of ethical and Fairtrade calendars available now and they are delicious, but personally I prefer the reusable Advent calendar. I sewed a reusable Advent calendar a couple of years ago and I'm going to love getting it out each year. I bought a kit that made it so simple to make. It took me about an hour at the sewing machine and will be used for years and years. It also means I can fill it with whatever I want!

There are lots of great tutorials on YouTube or Pinterest for hand-knitted, crocheted, felted or quilted Advent calendars that can come out year after year. Make something beautiful and special that will become a family heirloom. It doesn't need to be perfect. In fact, the more rustic the better! Whatever you make, I'm sure it will be treasured for years to come.

Here are some ideas for filling your reusable Advent calendar:

- A mini Fairtrade chocolate and a Bible verse.
- A different knitted, crocheted, felted nativity character, which over the course of the month you can place on display in a nativity scene.
- An activity for each day. This is a great one to do with the kids. It could be an opportunity to encourage children to help others or to spend time away from screens and connect as a family. If you're doing this with children, I suggest putting each activity in the night before, so you know it's something you can manage that day! If you're an adult doing an activity calendar, then choose ways to help others, get out into nature and also treat yourself. Ideas include going for a walk at lunchtime, baking cookies for you and a neighbour, making a hot chocolate and watching a Christmas film with a friend.
- A craft for each day. This is such a fun way to encourage you to slow down and make with your hands this Advent season. Many people enjoy hand-dyed yarn Advent calendars with a small skein of yarn each day. You then spend each evening knitting or crocheting a square/row of a blanket or shawl that will be done by Christmas. It's a great one for a bit of self-care and calm each evening in the lead-up to Christmas and often comes with minimal packaging.

The Advent candle

I come from a family that gathers around the kitchen table, and I think one of the reasons why my husband and I found it so easy to start our own home together is because he is also from a family that gathers around the kitchen table. For me, as a child, sofa dinners were a rarity saved only for the Christmas or Boxing Day evening buffet. Instead, we ate a homecooked meal at the dinner table each night, sharing about our day and catching up with each other away from screens. When mobile phones became the norm, the phrase 'No screens at the dinner table!' was heard nearly every evening. It was a screen-free zone. And still is.

Of course, as an adult I know now how lucky I am that this was the case. This connection in a family is important and something you have to work at. It doesn't always come easily. I do love a sofa dinner with a cosy episode of something after a long day, but sitting at the table each night is a wonderful way to connect and slow down this festive season.

One thing we used to do as a family to make this time of year more special was light an Advent candle. This was a numbered candle that sat in the middle of the table. Each evening we would light it and burn down one day. It added a certain level of ceremony and magic to December, reminding us of what we were moving towards.

Whether you live alone or in a house share or with family, I encourage you to take the twenty-four days of Advent as an opportunity to pause and reflect at the dinner table. Give yourself the luxury of sitting down each evening to a homecooked meal. If you're busy, try making some meals in advance to keep in the freezer, or start your day by throwing ingredients into the slow cooker for later. Light a candle and remember God's promise to the world. This is a great opportunity not just to catch up with the people you live with, whoever they might be, but also to chat about Christmas and what it's really about.

You could even go one step further and read a Bible verse from the Christmas story each night. There are plenty of devotionals online that split up the Christmas story for you into twenty-four chunks. What a beautiful way to end each day, remembering what you are really celebrating and looking forward to the time when Jesus will come again.

Seasonal celebrations: Christmas

For to us a child is born,
  to us a son is given,
  and the government will be on his shoulders.
And he will be called
  Wonderful Counsellor, Mighty God,
  Everlasting Father, Prince of Peace.
Of the greatness of his government and peace
  there will be no end.
He will reign on David's throne
  and over his kingdom,
establishing and upholding it
  with justice and righteousness
  from that time on and for ever.
The zeal of the Lord Almighty
  will accomplish this.
(Isaiah 9:6–7)

The hopes and fears of all the years are met in thee tonight.
(Phillips Brooks, 'O Little Town of Bethlehem', 1868)

Everyone seems to have their own version of the perfect Christmas. Some love to reminisce about the 1980s Christmas, with so much colour and tinsel you feel as if you've stepped inside Santa's workshop. Others, like my auntie Sarah, love the traditional Victorian Christmas like the one we see in *A Christmas Carol*. For me, it will always be a handmade and homegrown Christmas that feels best. One of my biggest inspirations for this time of year is Louisa May Alcott's novel *Little Women*: a simple Christmas, centred around home, church and generous giving. The beginning of this classic book is always a wonderful reminder of the true meaning of Christmas: love. 'For God so loved the world that he gave his one and only Son, that whoever believes in him shall not perish but have eternal life' (John 3:16).

The presents and the decorations are a way of reminding us of God's love and sacrifice. A reminder that we are so loved and are called to love others just as much. In all the busyness and the running around, it is important to repeatedly remember this truth.

A handmade and homegrown Christmas

There is nothing quite like a handmade Christmas. Weeks of work and effort go towards creating a beautiful home to celebrate the birth of Jesus. But there is no need to spend a lot of money. There are so many great cost-effective Christmas decoration tutorials out there on YouTube and Pinterest. Here are a few ideas to get you started.

Ribbons

When we had our first Christmas as a young married couple, we didn't have any decorations. I wanted to avoid all the plastic and glitter and instead choose carefully made keepsakes that would come out each year. The problem was, we couldn't afford to buy them all at once. We could only manage a few each year, so I started the tradition of trimming with ribbons.

Ribbons are a great decoration as they are relatively affordable and can be bought easily, or even collected over the year from presents and charity shops. I tie them on the candlesticks we have out all year on the mantelpiece, to make them look festive. I tie big bows to hang over mirrors and pictures, and smaller ones to attach to the branches of our tree. And a giant bow on the front door looks fantastic in place of a wreath. Ribbons are the decoration that keeps on giving.

One at a time

As I mentioned, we buy a couple of decorations each year, normally tree ornaments that are handmade, Fairtrade and sustainable. This way we have a memory from each year and slowly, over the eight years we've been married, we've created a collection of beautiful ornaments that don't harm the planet and will be used for many Christmases to come.

It is such a lovely treat each year to go out to a Christmas market and choose a beautiful handmade ornament to keep. Last year we found a handmade ceramic Christmas house in Germany. Every year it will come out and remind me of that special trip.

Handmade ornaments

As well as buying one or two special items a year, I also make a couple to add to the collection. These include things like tiny knitted sweaters and bobble hats, felted animals, salt-dough stars and macramé snowflakes.

Salt-dough star tutorial

It is so easy to make beautiful decorations with salt dough and it can involve the whole family.

Ingredients and equipment

- 200 g plain flour
- 100 g table salt
- 100 ml water
- Paint
- Twine

Method

1. Preheat the oven to lowest setting.
2. Line a baking sheet with baking paper.
3. Mix all the ingredients in a bowl until they form a dough.
4. Roll the dough out onto a floured surface, about 0.5 cm thick.
5. Cut out stars using a cookie cutter. It's nice to have a few different sizes.
6. Using a kebab stick, make a small hole in one point of each star.
7. Bake in the oven for around 3 hours, until solid.
8. Leave to cool and then paint, or you can leave them natural.
9. Thread a small length of twine or ribbon through the hole, and tie to make a loop.
10. Hang the decorations on your tree or around your home.

Tree alternatives

There have been a few years when we haven't had room for a Christmas tree, and I know it can be a big expense at this time of year. But there are lots of ways you can get that festive feeling without going the whole hog. A lot of places that sell Christmas trees will have off-cut branches that they often give out for free. These can be used in the following ways:

- *A traditional Scandinavian wall hanging* – Simply tie a ribbon or some twine to each end of a long branch and hang it on the wall. Then tie ribbons or lightweight ornaments to the small twigs on the branch.
- *A mantelpiece display* – Secure a mix of Christmas tree branches to your mantelpiece using twine, trying to hide it among the foliage. Add ribbons and decorations.

Edible Christmas decorations

We all love a chocolate on the Christmas tree in my family, but it can be so much fun to make your own edible Christmas decorations. Mini-gingerbread biscuit stars are a great one for baking a few days before Christmas and hanging on the tree (as with the salt-dough stars, use a cookie cutter, then a kebab stick for the hole, and thread with twine or ribbon).

Another option is to make a gingerbread house in the days leading up to Christmas. This is a lovely mindful activity that will slow the household down and fill it with the scent of Christmas. There are plenty of templates online and you could even have a go at making a gingerbread nativity!

Food

Christmas is one of my favourite times of year for food. I absolutely love all those spices and delicious fruits that we traditionally use in baking. But Christmas can also be a time of over-consumption and excess. It's easy to be swept up in the madness of it all, thinking you need twenty different packets of this and that, all because the shops are closing for one day.

I propose you slow it down. Focus on making and serving some delicious food you will really enjoy over the three main days. This is a great opportunity to do things differently. Choose seasonal local produce and maybe even serve up some of your own homegrown veggies. My husband has had many a failed attempt at growing Christmas sprouts, but one year we will manage it and what a treat it'll be! Last Christmas we were growing potatoes, but I know others who had parsnips and carrots waiting to be harvested on Christmas Eve.

Preparation

To ensure handmade, homegrown and slow Christmas food the key is to prepare. Try to do as much in advance as possible. My mum has always made the bread sauce and the cranberry sauce weeks before the big day, storing them in the freezer. This provides a way of having lovely homemade treats without all the stress of making them during the busy time.

This also works well for cordials, chutneys and infused spirits. Enjoy some days off quietly prepping delicious Christmas treats in October and November. You could also bake loaves to freeze or make up pizza dough, bread dough, scones and cookie dough for the freezer. Pizza dough is a great one to have in the freezer as it's easy to pull out and defrost on 27 December, when you've got a load of random leftovers that can be piled on as toppings. It is also a good idea to make sure you have room in your freezer for any leftovers after the big day, to avoid food waste.

Of course, if you're a fan of the Christmas cake or pudding, as I am, these are traditionally made in advance, famously on stir-up Sunday in November, and can be a lovely family activity to get you all looking forward to the season. There is something so mindful about regularly feeding a Christmas cake throughout Advent and anticipating the day it can be enjoyed as a family.

Gifts

Presents at Christmas have got a little out of hand over the years. I love waking up to a pile under the Christmas tree as much as the next person, but the amount of plastic waste from packaging, plus unwanted gifts, is extraordinary. In the UK alone it is estimated that over £42 million worth of unwanted gifts will make their way to landfill every year. This is totally avoidable with a little common sense and some thoughtful and slow gifting.

Of course, you don't have to buy gifts. You could choose not to if that is something you would like to do as a family. The other option is to agree to only buy for a select few, or even have a Secret Santa, to cut down on over-consumption. I know it might feel a bit awkward to have that conversation in the office or as a group of friends, but I bet there will be others sighing with relief that they don't have to spend more money or receive a gift they didn't really want in the first place.

For those who are very special in your life, whom you do want to buy a gift for, here are some alternative options that will help lower the impact this Christmas.

Handmade gifts

A well-made handmade gift is such a thoughtful present and has extra meaning to it, because you've spent time and effort making it especially for this person. It can also be a great opportunity to use up things you might already have in your crafting stash or use recycled materials from the charity shop. I like to make useful items – often ones that people can wear – especially when it comes to nephews and nieces!

Here are some ideas for handmade gifts:

- Knitted/crocheted hats, scarves, mittens and socks
- Apron
- Oven gloves
- Quilted potholders
- Christmas decorations
- Chutneys, jams, cordials, baked goods and infused spirits
- Dried flowers or floral wreath
- Soap
- Sourdough starter
- Seeds, plants, cuttings from the garden

Buy sustainable gifts

Buying useful and sustainable gifts that will be used again and again can really help to lower the impact on your purse and the planet this

Christmas. Focus on gifts that you know the person will use or, better yet, ask them or their loved ones what they would like, so you know you'll be getting it right.

Try to buy from shops that promote sustainable and ethical practices, or you could buy gifts second hand. There are so many gifts and toys in the charity shop at this time of year and they can be a cost-effective way to buy. I have also bought gifts from Vinted, Facebook Marketplace and eBay in the past.

Shop locally

Christmas is a good time to support your local high street. Books will always make a great Christmas gift, so why not buy from your local shop? If they don't have what you're looking for, they will nearly always be able to order it in for you.

Christmas markets are also a good place to pick up unique, thoughtful, sustainable and often handmade gifts from local small businesses and makers.

Cards and wrapping

The UK generates around 30% more waste over Christmas than at any other time during the year. This includes enough wrapping paper to cover Big Ben almost 260,000 times, and millions of Christmas cards that sadly aren't recycled and often end up in landfill. Choosing recyclable wrapping paper and Christmas cards can make a big difference and I love to make my own at Christmas time.

Handmade wrapping paper

It is best to do this well in advance of Christmas, so it has plenty of time to dry.

Equipment

- Recyclable brown paper
- Wooden Indian block prints
- Non-toxic acrylic paint
- Paint tray (I use an old takeaway container)
- Sponge
- Sponge mat or pad (this isn't essential but helps)

Method

1. Cut the paper to the right size for each of your presents.
2. Choose your colour and squirt a small amount onto your paint tray.
3. Place your paper over the sponge mat, then dab the colour onto your block print using the small sponge.
4. Start printing onto your paper, creating a design you like.
5. Allow plenty of time to dry before using to wrap gifts using paper tape.

You can finish off wrapping your gifts with recycled ribbons that you've kept over the year or found in the charity shop. Old yarn or twine works well too and if you really want to go to town, you can add a salt-dough decoration or a sprig of holly.

You can also use this method to create beautiful labels (again using brown paper labels that can be recycled) or Christmas cards (you can order recyclable brown cards online).

Another great option for gift labels is to save Christmas cards from the previous year to cut up. Simply punch a hole in one corner and write your message on the blank side.

Christmas Eve

The night before Christmas is such a magical time. Most of the work and preparation is done and it is time to sit in front of the fire and soak up the moment with friends and family. Some churches host their Christingle service on Christmas Eve (a fun one to attend with all the family), and of course there is Midnight Mass.

One tradition my husband and I have started recently is to read the Christmas story together on Christmas Eve. This is a good one to do with children, although you might prefer to use a children's Bible in that case. Use this time to take a breather before the madness of the big day. Immerse yourself in the story of the baby who came to save us all and remember just how much God loves you.

A prayer for Christmas Eve

Lord, thank you that you sent your Son for us. Thank you that you came as a tiny helpless baby to be our Saviour. Thank you that we get to celebrate this wonderful time together with friends and family. Lord, be with those who feel lonely. Would you help guide them towards others this Christmas. Lord, be with all of those struggling at this time of year. Would you surround them with your unfailing love. Lord, be here with our family as we remember your promise that one day you will come again and there will be more joy and light than even the best Christmas Day we can imagine. Amen.

Afterword

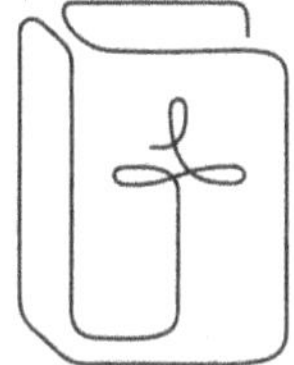

> Make it your ambition to lead a quiet life: you should mind your own business and work with your hands, just as we told you, so that your daily life may win the respect of outsiders and so that you will not be dependent on anybody.
> (1 Thessalonians 4:11–12)

This is one of my favourite verses in the Bible, and one which has led me to this new way of slow living. At a time when I felt I could do nothing, be nothing, it reminded me that I could still live a life pleasing to God. Becoming chronically ill in my mid-twenties meant a huge adjustment – a painful shedding of the life I had only just begun to build; a grieving for the life I thought I would lead. But God is always good. Even amid the struggle and the pain, and in that feeling of complete isolation and abandonment, God met me. And he showed me it could be good.

In her book *Keep a Quiet Heart*, Elisabeth Elliot writes: 'The secret of joy is Christ in me – not me in a different set of circumstances.'[12] And I know now what she means. Life is hard and we can try to pray away the pain and difficulty and stress, and sometimes God will answer us with exactly what we ask for. But even if he does – though for many of us he doesn't – it will never fully take away the hardship of this world. And so we must learn to find the beauty in the everyday. To find joy in every season – in the cold depths of winter, as well as the sweet colours of spring. To accept the painful shedding of leaves in autumn as much as we delight in the warm sunshine of summer.

Chronic illness slowed my life right down. It took me on paths I never thought I would end up on. It took away things I never thought I could survive without. But God, the ultimate author of all our stories, had a plan. He guided me towards a handmade, homegrown and slower life. A life more beautiful than I could have imagined for myself.

I don't know where you are in life right now. Perhaps, like me, you are in the midst of a health battle, or you are a new mum desperately trying to hold it all together or a young adult taking your first terrifying steps into the world and finding it overwhelming. Maybe you're retired, beginning that slowing down process but unsure of how to step off the hamster wheel. Whoever you are, I hope these pages have helped you find moments of calm as you begin to take stock, notice the simple joys and the beauty that is in every day.

I once heard John Mark Comer chatting on his podcast about a friend who had said, 'I do not want to miss the goodness of ordinary life.' And that is exactly what a handmade, homegrown and slow life is all about. Noticing the glimmers and romanticising the ordinary doesn't mean we don't struggle. It doesn't mean life isn't hard. And it isn't a substitute for having a relationship with God. But it can help us to connect with him. To find him in the overwhelming, fast pace of our days. It encourages us to take a step back, pause for a moment and feel that his presence is all around us. We all have so much to be grateful for.

This book was created to be a prompt that you can come back to again and again throughout the year. It is a manual with practical steps on how to live a handmade, homegrown and slow life. But it isn't just about following a list of tasks. This isn't a map to the perfect slow life. This is an invitation to get to know God more. Remember, it always starts with him. As we make with our hands, as we grow, as we live slowly and simply in the moment, we remember our Father, the creator of such beauty and the giver of simple joys throughout every single day.

The secret of joy is not growing vegetables, sewing clothes or hosting the best Christmas dinner party. God is our joy. Emmanuel. God with us.

So go out, live your best handmade, homegrown and slow life for God. Live quietly, make with your hands and find joy in the everyday. Because God is with us always.

Acknowledgements

This book could not have happened without the love, help and support of so many people. First, I'd like to thank my editor Lauren Windle, who responded with such excitement to my first email with a slightly mad idea to write a book that was 'cottagecore for Christians'. Straight from the off you just got what I was trying to do and the importance of the message. Thank you for your enthusiasm, support and belief that this was a book I could write that would speak to lots of people.

Second, I'd like to thank all those involved in the Bath Spa MA for Travel and Nature Writing (class of 2022!). Studying for two years under Stephen Moss and Gail Simmons, and alongside so many amazing writers, truly brought me back to life after some very difficult and unhappy years struggling with illness. The flexibility and support on the course allowed a chronically ill person to study well, find her way back to writing and grow in confidence to follow her dreams and become a freelance writer and published author. I will always be grateful for those amazing two years and the continued support I have received from you all. This book wouldn't have happened without you.

I'd also like to thank my wonderful church at the time of writing this. All of you at Chipping Norton Community Church have supported, loved and prayed with me through this process. Your support and belief in me have been so valuable. By the time this book is published we will have moved away, and I know I will be missing you all very much.

My family should also get a mention, both Burdett-Smiths and Bearns. Thank you for all your support while writing this book and for marketing it by telling all your friends. A special thanks to Mum and Dad for paying for all those creative writing lessons! And especially to my mum for taking me to church all those years ago as a baby and introducing me to faith.

I'd also like to say a big thank you to Sarah Corbett of the Craftivists – for your contribution to this book and for continuing to inspire people daily to take up their craft supplies and make a difference in this world.

And to my husband, the best man I know. All those years ago when we first started dating, I told you a secret I had never shared with anyone. I admitted that I had always wanted to be a writer. I wanted to quit my degree and finally follow my dreams to study creative writing. I didn't have the courage to do it alone. Your response, as ever, was filled with love and genuine belief in me. You told me to go after my dreams, and I did. That conversation and your continued belief in me is the only reason I have done all I have. You have supported me through illness, encouraged me through some of the hardest times and you never let me give up. Without you there would be no book. You are truly the best husband a girl could wish for.

Finally, I would like to thank all the people who have followed me on this journey: those who have subscribed to my YouTube channel, followed my Instagram page and subscribed to my Substack. Your support, love and community over the years have made all the difference. I appreciate every single one of you and I hope you love this book. It is really an extension of all I do online, and I couldn't have written it without your support. Thank you always.

Notes

1 Ralph Waldo Emerson, from his essay *Nature*, published in 1836.
2 John Mark Comer, *Garden City: Work, rest, and the art of being human* (Nashville: Thomas Nelson, 2017).
3 Edith Schaeffer, *The Hidden Art of Homemaking* (Carol Stream: Tyndale House, 1985). Copyright © 1971. Used by permission of Tyndale House Publishers. All rights reserved.
4 Anne Kirketerp, *Craft Pyschology: How crafting promotes health* (Hjørring: Mailand, 2024).
5 These words from Sarah, and those below, were given in personal interview during the writing of this book.
6 Frances H. Burnett, *The Secret Garden* (first published 1911).
7 Jane Milburn, Textile Beat blog, https://textilebeat.com/slow-clothing/#:~:text=Slow%20Clothing%20is%20a%20philosophy,outside%20what%20food%20does%20inside (accessed 11 March 2025). Used with kind permission.
8 Laura Ingalls Wilder, *A Family Collection: Life on the farm and in the country, making a home; the ways of the world, a woman's role* (published 1935).
9 This quote is commonly attributed to Louisa May Alcott, but the exact source is unknown.
10 Schaeffer, *The Hidden Art*.
11 Jamie Erickson, *Hygge: Creating a place for people to gather and the gospel to grow* (Chicago: Moody Publishers, 2022).
12 Elisabeth Elliot, *Keep a Quiet Heart* (Michigan: Revell, 2004).

Resources

Connect with me

YouTube – https://www.youtube.com/@RachelBearn
Instagram – @byrachelbearn
Substack – https://bearn.substack.com/
Pinterest – https://uk.pinterest.com/byrachelbearn/

1 Slow down

Jefferson Bethke, *To Hell with the Hustle: Reclaiming your life in an overworked, overspent, and overconnected world* (Nashville: Thomas Nelson, 2019).

John Mark Comer, *Garden City: Work, rest, and the art of being human* (Nashville: Thomas Nelson, 2017).

John Mark Comer, *The Ruthless Elimination of Hurry: How to stay emotionally healthy and spiritually alive in the chaos of the modern world* (London: Hodder & Stoughton, 2019).

Miranda Hart, *I Haven't Been Entirely Honest with You* (London: Michael Joseph, 2024).

Alex Howard, *Decode Your Fatigue: A clinically proven 12-step plan to increase your energy, heal your body and transform your life* (Carlsbad: Hay House, 2021).

Cathy Madavan, *Why Less Means More: Making space for what matters most* (London: SPCK, 2023).

Katherine May, *Wintering: The power of rest and retreat in difficult times* (London: Rider, 2020).

Georgia Varozza, *What the Amish Can Teach Us about the Simple Life: Homespun hints for family gatherings, spending less, and sharing your bounty* (Eugene: Harvest House, 2015).

2 By hand

Sarah P. Corbett, *How to Be a Craftivist: The art of gentle protest* (London: Unbound, 2017).

Sarah P. Corbett, *The Craftivist Collective Handbook: Projects, stories and methods for your gentle protest* (London: Unbound, 2024).

Riane Elise, *Quilting by Hand: Hand-crafted, modern quilts and accessories for you and your home* (London: Quadrille Publishing, 2021).

Anne Kirketerp, *Craft Psychology: How crafting promotes health* (Hjørring: Mailand, 2024).

Lindsey Newns, *Modern Crochet Style: 15 colourful crochet patterns for you and your home, including fun, sustainable makes* (Barnsley: White Owl, 2021).

Aneeta Patel, *Knitty-gritty: Knitting for the absolute beginner* (London: A & C Black, 2008).

Aneeta Patel, *Knitty-gritty: The next steps* (London: A & C Black, 2012).

Edith Schaeffer, *The Hidden Art of Homemaking* (Carol Stream: Tyndale House, 1985).

Tilly Walnes, *Love at First Stitch: Demystifying dressmaking* (London: Quadrille Publishing, 2014).

Tilly Walnes, *Make It Simple: Easy, speedy sewing projects to stitch up in an afternoon* (London: Quadrille Publishing, 2020).

3 Gardening

Dave Goulson, *The Garden Jungle or Gardening to Save the Planet* (London: Jonathan Cape, 2019).

Anna Greenland, *Grow Easy: Organic crops for pots and small plots* (London: Mitchell Beazley, 2021).

Jane Moore, *Planting for Wildlife: A grower's guide to rewilding your garden* (London: Quadrille Publishing, 2021).

Milli Proust, *From Seed to Bloom: A year of growing and designing with seasonal flowers* (London: Quadrille Publishing, 2022).

Huw Richards, *Veg in One Bed: How to grow an abundance of food in one raised bed, month by month* (London: DK, 2019).

Frances Tophill, *The Modern Gardener: A practical guide to gardening creatively, productively and sustainably* (London: Kyle Books, 2022).

Frances Tophill, *Rewild Your Garden: Create a haven for birds, bees and butterflies* (London: Greenfinch, 2020).

Alice Vincent, *Seeds from Scratch* (London: Coronet, 2020), audio book.

Sarah Wyndham Lewis, *Planting for Honeybees: The grower's guide to creating a buzz* (London: Quadrille Publishing, 2018).

4 Clothes

Patrick Grant, *Less: Stop buying so much rubbish: how having fewer, better things can make us happier* (Glasgow: William Collins, 2024).

Arounna Khounnoraj, *Visible Mending: Repair, renew, reuse the clothes you love* (London: Quadrille Publishing, 2020).

Safia Minney, *Slave to Fashion* (Oxford: New Internationalist, 2017).

Safia Minney, *Slow Fashion: Innovation through sustainability* (Oxford: New Internationalist, 2016).

Lucy Siegle, *To Die For: Is fashion wearing out the world?* (London: Fourth Estate, 2011).

Documentaries

Inside the Shein Machine: UNTOLD (Channel 4, 2022).

The True Cost (2015) by film-maker Andrew Morgan (available on YouTube).

5 Nature

Anna Deacon and Vicky Allan, *The Art of Wild Swimming: England & Wales* (Edinburgh: Black & White Publishing, 2021).

Tiffany Francis-Baker, *Dark Skies: A journey into the wild night* (London: Bloomsbury Wildlife, 2019).

Sarah Ivens, *Forest Therapy: Seasonal ways to embrace nature for a happier you* (London: Piatkus, 2018).

Lia Leendertz, *The Almanac: A seasonal guide to 2025* (Louisville: Gaia, 2024).

Robert Macfarlane and Jackie Morris, *The Lost Words* (London: Hamish Hamilton, 2017).

Emma Mitchell, *The Wild Remedy: How nature mends us – a diary* (London: Michael O'Mara Books, 2018).

Sholto Radford, *Walk: The path to a slower, more mindful life* (London: Quadrille Publishing, 2018).

6 Entertainment and community

John Mark Comer, *Practicing the Way: Be with Jesus, become like him, do as he did* (Colorado Springs: WaterBrook Press, 2024).

Catherine Price, *How to Break Up With Your Phone* (London: Trapeze, 2018).

7 Food

Becky Cole, *The Garden Apothecary: Transform flowers, weeds and plants into healing remedies* (London: Hardie Grant, 2022).

Hugh Fearnley-Whittingstall, *Eat Better Forever: 7 ways to transform your diet* (London: Bloomsbury, 2020).

Vanessa Kimbell, *The Sourdough School: The ground-breaking guide to making gut-friendly bread* (London: Kyle Books, 2018).

Michael Pollan, *In Defense of Food: An eater's manifesto* (London: Penguin, 2008).

Julius Roberts, *The Farm Table* (London: Ebury, 2023).

Madeliene Shaw, *Get the Glow: Delicious and easy recipes that will nourish you from the inside out* (London: Orion, 2015).

Chris van Tulleken, *Ultra-processed People: Why do we all eat stuff that isn't food ... and why can't we stop?* (London: Cornerstone Press, 2023).

Guy Watson, *Autumn and Winter: Cooking with a veg box* (Buckfastleigh: Riverford Organic Farms Ltd, 2015).

Guy Watson, *Spring and Summer: Cooking with a veg box* (Buckfastleigh: Riverford Organic Farms Ltd, 2015).

John Wright, *The Forager's Calendar: A seasonal guide to nature's wild harvests* (London: Profile Books, 2020).

The *River Cottage Handbook* (London: Bloomsbury). There are currently eighteeen of these in the series, by various authors.

For sourdough recipes check out: https://www.farmhouseonboone.com/ (accessed 3 March 2025).

8 Home

Jamie Erickson, *Holy Hygge: Creating a place for people to gather and the gospel to grow* (Chicago: Moody Publishers, 2022).

Bea Johnson, *Zero Waste Home: The ultimate guide to simplifying your life by reducing your waste* (New York: Scribner Book Company, 2013).

Rebecca Sullivan, *The Art of the Natural Home: A room by room guide* (London: Kyle Books, 2017).

Meik Wiking, *The Little Book of Hygge: Danish secrets to happy living* (New York: William Morrow & Co., 2017).

Advent and Christmas

Lucy Brazier, *Christmas at River Cottage* (London: Bloomsbury, 2017).

Angela Maynard, *The Art of Gifting Naturally: Simple handmade projects to create for friends and family* (London: Hardie Grant Books, 2022).